VESTED INTERESTS

How rarely Reason guides the stubborn Choice,
Rules the bold Hand, or prompts the suppliant Voice. . .

---from Samuel Johnson's
The Vanity of Human Wishes

Vested Interests
Essays and Fantasies

by

Ralph A. Raimi

Published by the author at
46 Glen Ellyn Way
Rochester, New York 14618
1982

ISBN 0-9609370-0-5

Printed in
Rochester, New York,
United States of America

To my wife, Sonya

Note

Acknowledgement is hereby gratefully made to the original publishers of many of the pieces in this book:

To the New York Times, for *Learning Twice,* which appeared in its Educational Supplement of 26 April 1981 under the title *Twice-Told Tale: The Joy of Teaching,* ©1981 The New York Times Company, reprinted by permission.

To the American Jewish Committee and Commentary, for *Vested Interests,* which appeared in *Commentary,* Vol. 58, No. 3, September 1974.

To the Gannett Rochester Newspapers and the *Rochester Democrat and Chronicle*, in which, under various headlines and on the dates mentioned appeared the Op-Ed pieces reprinted in this book under the titles *Feminist Linguistics* (7/19/74), *Minimum Wages* (12/13/74), *The Middle-man* (4/28/75), *Name Discrimination* (9/1/75), *Approved Publishers* (4/18/77), *Selling Russian Jews* (7/7/78), *Cultural Exchanges* (7/17/78), *Helsinki Mathematical Congress* (9/6/78), *Why Study a Foreign Language?* (9/12/79), *Defending the Academy* (1/11/80), *A Wineglass in the Teeth* (12/13/80), and *Decline of the English Language Isn't 'Nyoo'* (1/4/78), all reprinted by permission.

To the University of Rochester and the *Rochester Review*, for *The Detroit Answer* (Fall, 1977), *Relevance* (Spring, 1972), *Noblesse Oblige* (Summer, 1977), and *A Proposal Concerning Conscience* (Winter, 1969).

To the University of Rochester and its student newspaper *The Campus-Times,* for *Opium of the People* (1/17/74 and 1/21/74), *The Triumph of Socialism* (2/5/73), and *Letter From Vancouver, B.C.* (11/1/74).

To the University of Rochester and two ephemeral student publications of the year 1972, for *Magic* and *On Liberty.*

Contents

Contents (Continued)

Introduction

1. The most famous mathematician of the 19th Century was not Gauss, Riemann, or Lobachevsky; it was Charles L. Dodgson, the author (though under another name) of *Alice in Wonderland.* Nonmathematicians are sometimes surprised to learn that Lewis Carroll was a mathematician by trade, but no mathematician could read ten pages of *Alice* without recognizing the point of view.

As a professor of mathematics myself, I have something in common with Reverend Dodgson. Of course, the essays and fantasies in this book do not really resemble anything in the works of Lewis Carroll, but they do--I assure you--have in common with his writings the mathematician's point of view. Whether this is as visible in my writing as in his I must leave it to readers to decide. With this comment I hope I am making it easier to decide my way.

2. This collection contains some 'dated' material. I wish I could have published some of it while it was timely, especially *Letter From San Francisco,* an isolated bit of history not rounded off at the ends. Its far end, however, contains a prediction that is now coming true, I believe; maybe that was worth waiting for.

The Majority Opinion contains the verdict I should have had the sense--and courage--to write when I was in 1967 the Chief Justice (of a sort) in a student disruption case at the University of Rochester. Alas, it took me a year or two to reach this much understanding of the issues. I will never get over my shame at having been taken in, even briefly, by the apologists for zealotry.

3. The truth-fiction standing of these pieces should be clarified for the record. The *Newspaper Pieces,* the *Learned Controversy,* and the *Pessimistic Essays* (Chapters V—VII) are exactly what they say they are: opinion mixed with fact, totally without fantasy or fiction. Likewise, *Opium of the People, Letter From San Francisco,* and *Actual Malice* are plain reporting and comment.

All the rest of the book contains fiction or fantasy at least in part, though *Forty Years in the Desert* is very close to a true story about my real Uncle Zalman, whose name I retained for memory's sake while changing and inventing some other names and events. Things like *Relevance* and *Prize-Day Ceremony* are obviously pure fiction, while things like *The Detroit Answer* are as plainly rooted in experience though fiction in detail. Any reader who has carefully studied Chapter VI and done all the exercises should be able to recognise the mixtures for what they are. Just the same, I wish to warn my personal friends that *Husband and Wife* and *Noblesse Oblige* are 100% pure fiction, however much some of the scenery (like the Brighton Recycle Center) looks real. Nothing, on the other hand, could be realer than *Mode d'Emploi,* though the monologue itself never occurred.

4. The dates which appear on the chapter title pages are of the years in which the respective articles were written.

Rochester, N.Y.
12 June 1982

Chapter I: **Domestic Observations**

The Detroit Answer

MY CHILDREN have recently given a name to a mode of conversation perhaps well known but, I think, worthy of explicit description. They call it the Detroit Answer, because they were most struck with it while visiting relatives in Detroit. It is not unknown in our own home, of course, but since it is plainly an evil we like to give it an out-of-town name.

One of the exchanges that gave rise to our analysis went like this:

Q. *Is this Grandma's hairbrush?*

A. *You can use it, dear.*

There seems to be nothing but goodwill in the reply. The respondant is evidently being generous, 'generous to a fault' as it is sometimes said. As it happened, my daughter did not want to brush her hair, but rather wanted to return the brush (which she had found on the floor) to the proper dresser-top in her grandparents' room.

Aunt Flora would have been hurt to have been told to stop being presumptuous and answer the question, so my daughter went on, mildly,

Q. *No, thanks; I only wanted to put it away. Where does it go?*
to which Aunt Flora replied,

A. *Oh, you don't have to, darling.*

More generosity, another answer to an unasked question while the asked question remained unanswered.

Coming home we played car-games with the Detroit Answer, recollecting some and improving others. The sport lasted for months; I kept a file.

Q. *How do you turn on this television set?*

A. *Don't play it now.*

Q. *How long do you cook hot dogs?*

A. *You boil them.*

Q. *Yes, but how long do you boil them, like the ones here?*

A. *We're not having them tonight.*

Q. *How come you got five World Almanacs?*
A. *You want one?*

Q. *Which book did you give him?*
A. *It was my book.*

Q. *Où se trouve l'Eglise de St. Germain des Prés?*
A. *Je ne suis pas du quartier.*

The Detroit Answer is a certain kind of non-response to a direct question, given in the form of a response. It is in fact a response to some other question, the question the respondant thinks the questioner is really asking, or at any rate ought to have been asking.

Q. *What time will dinner be?*
A. *Just as soon as I can manage it.*

Here a direct answer might be "6:30 or so." The answer actually given was the answer to another question, perhaps "How come dinner's never ready on time around here?" To such ill-temper there really is no answer except a denial of fault, which is implicit in the Detroit Answer given.

Another example: I am in a restaurant and haven't seen my waitress in some time. I ask another waitress, who happens to be passing by,

Q. *Can you get our waitress, please?*
A. *That's not my table.*

It may be that I didn't ask my question loudly enough, but I doubt it. Nothing would convince that waitress that I have any right to her attention. The question she is really answering is

Q. *Waitress, am I entitled to talk to you?*

Firm in her mind is the answer "No", accompanied by sufficient reason. She would give the same answer if I asked her to marry me. Her ears have no function in my direction.

The undercurrent of ill-will here has this in common with the dinner-time example: it is linked to a strong sense of injustice, perhaps a long history of injustice. In fact, there is one Detroit Answer which could have been given to both questions, and which would exhibit most clearly what is in the mind of the respondent:

A. *It's not my fault. Whatever you're asking (and can't you see I have no time to go into subtleties?), it is not my fault. It is not I who made dinner late; I didn't hide your waitress. Take*

care of your own troubles, and don't add to mine.

Indeed, the harried housewife or waitress may have justice on her side, and the questioner may not really be as innocent as he sounds. Perhaps he does nag his wife day in and day out for her deficiencies, as he conceives them, and his question is a disingenuous fault-finding. He knows he is not entitled to complain about dinner, or at least that he hasn't enough information about the circumstances to be sure he is right about complaining. So he pretends not to complain while yet conveying his disapproval; to his wife it is therefore clear that he deserves the Detroit Answer. She hears his intent, not his words.

If, on going to work in the morning he asks her,

Q. *What time are we due at the Harrison's dinner?*

she will probably answer

A. *6:30.*

If, on the other hand, it is 6:15 p.m. and she is fuming before the mirror trying to get her hair-piece in place, and he asks the same question, with the same words and intonation, he will likely get

A. *I'm getting dressed as fast as I can.*

The chances are that she is right to answer so, for his question at that time could have served no purpose beyond irritation. Nothing depended on it, after all; when her hair is done they will leave, and not a minute before.

But if she is right in interpreting his tone, it doesn't follow that she is right to escalate the conflict by pointing up that tone with her answer. However many pins she has in her mouth,

A. *6:30*

is surely best. Even if his question had no purpose but to annoy, what has she gained with her plea of faultlessness? He, if he is so disposed, will not allow that plea, but will (pretending bland innocence all the while) come back with another attack. He may even believe in his innocence, as in the following scene.

Father: Where is the soap?

Mother: Oh--*I'm* sorry; I thought there was some.

Father: O.K., but where do you keep the soap?

Mother: What do you mean, 'Keep the soap?' Do you think I'm hiding it from you? I just told you I didn't mean to take it away. I'll get it for you now.

Father: No--don't get up; just tell me where you--where the soap--

uh, I mean, do you keep it in the basement or on the pantry shelf? I'm on my way downstairs...

Mother: Oh, no; I'm about done mending your sweater anyway. I'll be right up with it. (sings) Oh, soap, oh soapy soap-soap, oh soapy soap-soap for daddums. (Calls downstairs) Linda dear (this is the daughter, who is swaying to a rather loud recording in the living room), Linda! Run down to the laundry room and get Daddy a cake of soap.

Daughter: Wha? (She has heard the question, but only barely, over the music. Her mother really should have come down to talk to her, instead of shouting. It would have been perfectly possible *not* to have understood, given the circumstances.)

Mother: LINDA!

Daughter: YES, MOTHER?

Mother: I *told* you to get your father a cake of soap. He's waiting!

Daughter: But I didn't hear you. Where do you keep the soap?

Mother: Oh never mind. Go back to your music; I'll get it myself.

Daughter: But mother, all I said was...(Here the father passes them both as he goes downstairs to the laundry room, in a silence which contains all the questions and answers in the house.)

Mother: (to daughter) See? Why can't you listen, instead of making your father run downstairs after a long day at the office? (Calls out to Father) Wait a minute, dear; I'm coming right down...

The mirror image of the Detroit Answer is the Detroit Question. Here the questioner does not ask what he needs to know, but instead asks a prior question, usually relating to the schedule or the convenience of the person addressed. The idea is that if convenience is established the real request is not a genuine demand; it costs no moral debt. In short, a Detroit Question is one which deserves a Detroit Answer; in fact, it can hardly be given any other.

For example, the questioner wants a ride downtown later in the afternoon, and so,

Q. Do you have a lot of work today?

A. Well--I dunno. I got to go over that review article, but it isn't long. Jack might come over. . .why?

Q. Well, I didn't want to interfere with your afternoon.

A. But I don't *know;* why?

Q. Whattya mean, you don't know? I just asked a simple question. I don't like to make you run errands for me when you've got something important to do. If Gladys were home I wouldn't have to ask you.

A. Ask me what?

Q. Not if you're too busy, darling.

Mode d'Emploi

THE MAIN thing about the dishwasher is you got to wash the dishes before you put them in,not after you take them out, because by then it's all baked on and the work is twice as much. Like spinach. That really sticks on; if you don't get every speck of it off to start with you might as well get a chisel to it when it's dry.

Coffee, too. The best way I found is to rub my fingers over a bar of soap and then around the inside of the cup. You can see the stain running out in the rinse. Then put it in the dishwasher and you're all set.

Rice is another one to watch out for; it bakes on like plaster in the dry cycle. Actually rice isn't so bad, in case you forget, because it will chip off pretty clean, but you have to watch for it because it's white and you might miss it when you're putting the dishes away.

Now pots are a whole problem of their own. Even if the spray could reach them, they take up a lot of room you probably need for something else. But if you're going to put pots in the dishwasher anyhow, you'd better be specially careful about the ones with straight sides. Not the bowls--they're all right, usually--but the saucepans. With the square bottoms--not square but sharp, if you see what I mean. Round bottoms, but sharp at the edges. When you get a pot like that, the water from the washing spray doesn't reach up along the sides, no matter how you put it, bottom shelf or top.

So the thing is to steel-wool it first, or use a stainless-steel pad. Made of shavings. Use soap and scrub the bottom edges especially, and then you can put it most anywhere. Bottom shelf, probably.

Glassware is easy. It comes out shinier than if you dried it yourself on a clean towel. That's where the dishwasher really pays off. Except if you have cups or tumblers with a dimple in the bottom. On the outside bottom, like a French wine bottle, the bottom isn't flat but has a sort of bulging-in, curved. Like you can hold the bottle upside down and you still have a sort of cup there.

Well, some glasses are like that, tumblers with heavy bottoms usually, but also the kind of coffee cups that have little round rims on the bottom that fit in the middle of the saucer not to slip around.

Now you get a tumbler or cup like that on the top shelf straight upside-down, the rinse water will end up collecting in the dimple--it'll stay there right through the dry cycle. So then, when you pull out the top shelf to put them away, they'll all bump against each other and clank like, and the water in the little pools in the dimples will get shook out and run down their sides and get on the dishes below, and the silver, and you'll have to wipe them all.

Well, there's no reason for that. You can get around it this way: you load the glasses in very carefully so they're not straight up and down. Just a little tilt is usually enough to do it, because the dents aren't very deep, so with a little tilt they won't hold any water in the first place. If of course if you laid them down it would be even better, but then the insides wouldn't get washed; you wouldn't want to do that unless you washed the insides first. Even then, laying down takes up too much room. And some of the rinse water might take to staying on their insides.

But you can't tilt the glasses (or cups) exactly as far as you need on every machine. Some dishwashers don't have the right shape shelf for that, or the prongs point too straight. It might depend on how wide the glasses are whether you can do it. Partitions too, they come different ways. If you get so you can only put the glasses in straight upside down, or laying down, you got a problem. Here's what I do.

First, I put them in fairly straight, and run the washer. Then when the last rinse is over and the dial clicks over to *dry*, and the coil starts hotting up in the bottom, I open up the washer and jerk out the top tray, maybe in and out a couple of times. The glasses rattle against each other and the water in the pools jumps out and runs down their sides like I said, only the difference is that this time you still have the drying to go. The water gets on the bottom dishes and coils and all, but that doesn't matter. You just push in the shelf and close the door and let the *dry* cycle continue on. There won't be any pools left at the end, you'll see.

Of course sometimes you can't be there to do this at just the right time. If you go away for a while, then there's only one thing you can do when you come back. You open the dishwasher carefully and pull out the top tray very slowly so as not to disturb the little pools of rinse water. Take a clean dish towel, or paper towel, and crumple it up and touch it to the bottom of every glass that needs it. This goes pretty fast, even if you twist the cloth a little every time to sort of polish it up. Then when you unload there isn't any dripping.

I hate to do that, though, because it's like I wasn't using the dishwasher for all its worth. I mean, if you have to dry the dishes yourself, what's the thing for?

One other thing. If you're washing some plastic refrigerator boxes, square or round doesn't matter, with the tops that press on all around or even the tops that screw on, though they are heavier and so don't flip as easy, sometimes the spray from the bottom of the dishwasher will make them flip over. That's because they are not as heavy as cups and glasses. When you put them against the spray it's like a sail or a water wheel, and half the time they come back upside down from what they should be and they will hold more water than the glasses with the dimple bottoms.

Even soapy water because there will be so much, and even bits of food from off any dishes you maybe forgot to wash before loading them in. So when you pull out the top shelf you'll spoil the whole load. I mean, the garbage and dirty water will get all over the dishes on the bottom shelf, or whatever you got down there. Pans too.

You can not fix that by putting the plastic boxes on the bottom shelf, because they melt near the coil on *dry*. There's really only one thing you can do. You wedge all the plastic things between whatever you've got on top, so as to hold them in place. It might take some rearranging, but if you think what you are doing you can do it. You might have to lay a pot cover on top of some of the ones you couldn't wedge in, to keep them from jumping up.

But if you have a lot of glasses up there all tilted a little bit the way I said before you will have to be careful not to disturb their angle, so I can't give you a hard and fast rule on how you have to do it. You'll just have to use your initiative.

Wife and Husband

THE MODERN homemaker is educated in everything but homecraft. She is an artistic type, handy with sewing-machine, potter's wheel, hand loom; she binds books in half-calf, makes her own draperies, ashtrays and dresses; but these things are not housekeeping.

A clean and orderly house is improved, to be sure, by new curtains, new paint, superior gadgetry, artistic design; but a dirty and disorganized house is only the more depressing: carefully placed Danish furniture (covered with crayons and potato chips), grey and white Vinyl tile kitchen floor (knee-deep in carrot shavings, cat food, onion skills, Spanish olive oil, Colombian coffee grounds), delightfully gay red and white striped bathroom (hair on the sink, combs, rubber bands, half-squeezed toothpaste tube, smeared mirror, bathtub ring, towels everywhere).

The lamp that stands on the long cabinet in the living room is placed two-fifths of the distance from the near end; the tiny Rembrandt etching is on the wall behind the farther end, where the top opens for the stereo turntable. The long cabinet itself, in teak, has a fine oil finish and would glow beautifully in contrast to the bright lampshade, were it not for the children's wooly gloves and lunchbox dripping with melting snow, and the sheets of muddy creative art brought home from school. The colors of mud and these random articles were not in our homemaker's mind when she planned the room.

Nor are they in her mind now, even looking at them, as she comes in from the kitchen. She sees the polished wood, the lampshade, the etching just as she saw them when first she put them there. They will be forever beautiful in her mind, forever perfect. An unexpected guest arrives; she looks around hurriedly and says, 'Excuse the terrible mess, but I just didn't get around to dusting this morning (ha, ha)'. She removes a glove or lollipop before pouring coffee. But this doesn't mean she *sees* the dust or disorder. She knows about them just as she knows about poverty in India; sometimes she tries to do something about one or the other, but not from inner need.

Her husband's study, on the other hand, is on her mind constantly.

For one thing, the walls are entirely too dull a brown---well, beige, actually, but old and dingy. The curtains are *wrong* (they used to be in the living room of the old house), and won't match when the walls are repainted. The easy chair desperately needs recovering. Altogether the room is a horror and a drag on her mind.

But in fact she never visits the place. Her husband spends many evenings there in peace and quiet. His books are on their shelves; his desk-top is clear. His pens, writing paper, typewriter, current work and correspondence are all in their appointed places, and since he washes out the translucent bowl of his standing lamp once in a while the light is pleasant and easy.

Sometimes he removes his shoes at the door, so as not to crunch into his retreat the cornflakes and apple-cores sticking to them from his trip up the stairs. In stockinged feet he feels the cool smooth floor, which he sweeps in secret, and is happy.

Chapter II: **On Education**

Opium of the People

MY BROTHER taught me to read and my parents taught me how to cross the Detroit streets safely. With these two skills well established by the time I was seven years old--this was 1931--I could with profit and safety walk to the Main Branch of the Detroit Public Library each Saturday morning.

Apart from the influence of my brother, and (naturally) of those librarians who had selected the holdings in the first place, my reading was random. The library had been there for years; many tastes were represented. King Arthur, The Steadfast Tin Soldier, d'Artagnan and, as the years wore on, tales of Copernicus and Louis Pasteur. I learned how it was to have been a Plebe at West Point in 1902, and a classmate of Hungry Smeed at Lawrenceville. Fu Manchu, Tarzan, Sorhab and Rustam were equally real with Teddy Roosevelt and Robert of Sicily.

My choices had nothing to do with Education, which my parents and I assumed was the province of the public schools I attended. Not until deep into high school, and mainly later, did my recreational reading intersect my formal education. Mostly they were in opposition. I would sometimes read stealthily in class while a lesson was going on around me.

Self-teaching, with or without a brother, is bound to leave gaps. I didn't hear of Transubstantiation until college. Bad luck, that's all; if my hand had plucked the right book from the shelf one Saturday morning I might have learned Sanskrit--who knows? I chose by color and title, and one can aspire to only so much in the way of luck.

Surely one can hope for more in an organized school, especially a high school. I went to the Central High School, 1938-41, five or six hours a day and in the flower of my intellectual growth. It was a middle-class neighborhood, not a black-board jungle; there was no war, no hunger, no racial strife there. How many useful things I could have learned, with joy and with ease: Greek, the history of China and the game of Go, for example. Alas, of these I still know next to nothing. In my adult years I suppose I could have looked into them more than in fact I have, but by then at some expense to something else. At Central I could have learned them at no cost at all. What *did* I learn then?

I attended among others, classes labelled history, economics, civics and physics. I name these four because I have a vivid recollection of a characteristic feature of each, a feature of instruction which I believe characterized all subjects taught me at that time: a listing.

(1) Economics: The Four Properties of Gold, The Three Funtions of Money.
(2) History: The Three Causes of the Civil War, The Seven Provisions of the Treaty of Versailles.
(3) Civics: The Capitals of the 48 States, The Three Kinds of City Governments.
(4) Physics: The Three Methods of Heat Transfer.

Consider gold. It is (a) Valuable,
(b) Divisible,
(c) Portable, and
(d) Enduring

For these reasons, I was taught, gold is used as Money. Granite and iron fail to satisfy (a) and (c), or at least no given quantity of (say) iron used as coin can simultaneously be both valuable and portable; hence civilized people don't use iron coins. Platinum, on the other hand, so well satisfies (a) that it can hardly be divisible (b) without danger of loss. So it went. (It could have been amusing to think of substances satisfying the various subsets of these four properties. Some might say *love* satisfies all but (d). We didn't play games with our lists at Central, however.)

The economics teacher insisted a good deal on these four properties of gold. The class was called on in alphabetical order, to stand up and recite the list of the day (one list could last several days) with precision and understanding. The reader must not think this list was a minor matter, a passing comment in an otherwise substantial book or course. Much ancillary and illustrative material was offered by both teacher and textbook, concerning these essential properties of gold.

We were told that some ancient (hence silly) lands used large bronze discs, too heavy to carry, as currency. Such a violation of (c) *portable* was its own punishment. I received the distinct impression that these people (they were either Neanderthal men or Etruscans, I forget which) walked lopsided, and in any case not far from home.

How many tales of wampum have I not heard? I had courses in wampum beginning in kindergarten, and while the formal study of braves, squaws, and Happy Hunting Grounds is usually completed by the fifth grade I am quite sure wampum got into the high school economics lesson of which I have been speaking.

There was a second list, *The Three Functions of Money,* essential to the first. You know of course that money is:

(α) A Standard of Value,

(β) A Medium of Exchange, and

(γ) A Standard for Deferred Payments.

One cannot forget this and understand the four properties of gold, after all. Were it not for deferred payments (γ), the property (d) *enduring* would hardly be memorable or necessary, for example.

I'm sorry I don't still have that textbook; I must have sold it in June of 1940 to some student who would take the same class the following fall. June, 1940! Gold had not been used as currency in America for the previous seven years, or since. What was I saying, what was my teacher listening to, when I stood up beside my desk to recite these idiocies?

My economics teacher was named Mr. Minton (believe it or not); he and I had both lived through the closing of the banks in 1933, a period when the City of Detroit, totally bankrupt, paid its school teachers in 'scrip', a currency without backing and which still did the job. Did he think of this when he drilled us on the portability of gold? I doubt it. The properties of gold were schoolbook truths, independent of the world outside. They too were a sort of currency. They travelled in a closed system from textbook to teacher to student to exam, and reentered the system when some particularly malleable student became a teacher in his turn, and wrote a textbook in careful improvement of those which had made him the man he was.

Still, that about the gold was not so entirely wrong. It had probably been cribbed in twelve relays from Adam Smith or Jean-Baptiste Say, so it is not surprising that a germ of truth remained. I later learned that value, divisibility and portability are in fact a sensible list of demands to make money, even if durability is asking perhaps more than modern governments committed to inflation can provide; and that while there isn't enough gold around to serve the whole world in this way, a "promise to pay" will serve as well. It is a stable government's promise to pay which we have used as currency since

1933, and in effect earlier too; even when we called it gold it was in fact sometimes green and crinkly, and sometimes only a rubber ink stamp of a bank teller.

I have no recollection that Mr. Minton appreciated all this. Even if he had, and had been willing to substitute the list of properties for the actual yellow metal in our classroom discussions, whatever would he have made of the word "value"? Even in a correct formulation, the list exhibits what must be the most trivial or tautological aspects of the science of money, but this was no disqualification from its use in Central High School during the Battle of Britain. There, at Central, it was an island of certitude. At the end of the day we could know we had done our job, all of us, who remembered (a) through (d) in the right order, and spoke them with expression, like an Edgar Guest poem in the morning's Detroit Free Press.

I know there were Three Causes of the Civil War (i.e. the American "war between the states") but I can only remember *Sectionalism.* It is hard to quarrel with that one. They might as well have listed *Soldiers* or *Secession.* Come to think of it, as I remember that textbook it was perfectly capable of listing secession as a cause, but I just don't remember. It must be that I wasn't called on to recite during that particular lesson, which took place in the Durfee Intermediate School, 9th Grade, sometime in 1937.

What is easier to remember is that *Slavery* was not a cause of the Civil War, or at any rate not a certified cause of the 9th Grade Durfee School civil war. Our teacher was quite insistent about it. When called on to recite the causes of the Civil War, or if asked about it on a State Proficiency Examination (or whatever), we were not--repeat, *not*--to list slavery.

Now the 9th grade is farther back in my memory than the 12th and it is a bit harder to visualize the textbooks and the general form of classroom procedure. There was a list, I am sure of that, and the causes were certainly three, but that part about slavery may have been due to our teacher and not the book. I believe the teacher was trying to be deep instead of superficial, and hoping to take us behind the scenes, as it were. *Slavery*--hideous as it was--was only a symptom of some deeper malaise, I bet.

Detroit was still in the grip of the Depression, and Marxist ideals vied with trade-unionism in portraying the economic royalists as the cause of all our ills. I heard it at home and it must have penetrated the schools. Even if "surplus value" wasn't trotted out in the open, everyone was affected by the notion that all causes were deeper than they appeared. Marx and Freud are an infestation to this day, after all, and their fundamental message is actually neither economic nor psychiatric, it is that things are really the opposite of what they seem. Thus the downgrading of "slavery" in favor of the more general and more resonant.

Except then for *sectionalism* ("deep") and *slavery* ("superficial") I recall nothing I learned in school about the Civil War. Nothing in "social studies," that is. In music class we sang "Mahty Lak a Rose" and "Massa's In De Col' Col' Groun'." At home over the next few years I read *Uncle Tom's Cabin, Gone With The Wind* and *Black Boy*. These things didn't touch the Civil War I had learned about in that Gothic and brick school building; they were part of some second Civil War that I gradually had to put together in my own mind and that I am still far from fully appreciating.

Oh yes--one vignette. There was a horrible day when I was convinced for a while that one of the approved causes of the Civil War was *Coalition*. It happened this way. The teacher began the class by mentioning the Three Causes, and while my attention wandered she wrote some of them, maybe all Three, something at any rate, on the blackboard. That is how I remember it. Probably I heard the chalk on the board but was looking out of the window. Coming out of my daze then, I focussed on the chalked word COALITION, printed on what I have since come to realize must have been a different part of the blackboard from the one she had just been using.

Her voice washed over me as I studied the word. Coal? That went with Oil and Gas, and the unit on Transportation and Communication. Probably the teacher was saying words like Secession or Sectionalism, only vaguely according with the word that was bemusing me. I looked at it a long long time.

Coming home that night I looked it up in the dictionary and it was still a puzzle. I may have spent a fevered night trying to reconcile the day's experiences, maybe not. Only gradually, over the years, have I become certain that COALITION was an artifact of the classroom, a word left over from an earlier class and not at all, not even marginally, not even negatively like *Slavery,* a cause of the Civil War.

Did I say *certain?* That is too strong. No, there is simply no telling. It has been thirty-five years now, and not one of them has passed without my turning to the matter in some mentally idle moment, trying to figure out a way to make *coalition,* or some brief phrase containing the word, a duly listed cause of the War Between The States. There is no way to make it an *obvious* cause, to be sure, but (as I have explained) we didn't deal in obvious causes in those days.

The Capitals of the 48 States! I knew them once. Now there are 50 but I'm not sure about the new ones. Honolulu? Anchorage? Maybe some of the old ones have changed too, or is that against the law?

I knew Lansing, Michigan, of course, since I had been there, and lived in Michigan anyhow. I don't know why *you* should remember it though. Any New York child who thinks Detroit is the capital of Michigan shows thereby a certain understanding of Detroit and of Michigan which I count all to the good, in fact.

One asset this list of 48 had was that it was natural. It was in some sense a false lesson to be taught the Civil War had precisely three causes, not two, not seven, but there was no denying the forty-eightness of this particular list, or its correctness. The only question is, why?

Progressive educators and modern parents were forever asking, even in my day, why one had to learn this or that foolish thing: Latin (a dead language), algebra (not true-to life). They didn't really ask--they knew the answer in advance. There *was* no valid reason, if you were modern about it. Even my teachers (the younger ones) often commented in class--as they had been taught in Teacher's College--on the deadening effect of learning the dates of events in history.

So I grew up among classmates who couldn't place Julius Caesar and Napoleon in correct chronological order. That I could do so was an accident of my reading, but no such accident taught me Latin. I regret it to this day. Almost everything whose utility was under such attack in those days--algebra, Latin, dates, memorized poems--has seemed to me as an adult to be of enormous utility, while the list of 48 capitals, which everyone must have considered very practical knowledge, like a visit to the firehouse, now seems as much a waste of time as ever.

I can think of one interesting lesson to be drawn from that list, but it was a lesson probably not appreciated by my teachers. The thing about our Capitals is that they are not necessarily, indeed very seldom, the most important cities of their respective states. This fact was mentioned in my class, but no explanation was given. In fact, nobody even said why this fact was remarkable.

If my teacher had mentioned Paris, London, Madrid, Rome, Berlin, Moscow, Copenhagen, Stockholm, Athens, Cairo, Bagdad and Tokyo, and then gone on to mention Albany, Lansing and Sacramento, we would at least have seen there was a puzzle buried somewhere between the two lists. These lists call attention to a deep distinction between the New World and the old: Here, we set up our maps and governments *before* a State began its history, rather than after, as in the rest of the world. Something to ponder, something we have evidence for before our eyes, but it wasn't in the book, not on the exam.

How could it have been taught, after all? We would have had to invoke European history and culture, which was taught in a different grade. And how would it have looked on an examination? "Fill in the blanks in the following sentence: The States of the United States were mostly created_____their history began, rather than____, so that . . ."

Not such a good question, is it? Also the explanation is only partial. After all, in some cases (Michigan among them) it was plain from the beginning which city would be preeminent, from its position on a waterway in most cases, yet the Capital was deliberately placed elsewhere. Why? In Europe, of course, the Capital was where the King was, and everything else followed: Cathedrals, artists, law courts, trade. Why did Michigan *want* it otherwise?

The more I think about it, the more I have to draw on my knowledge of the facts of history, the flavor of social history, the currents of war and diplomacy, the theories of American republicanism. To get up a respectable lecture would take work as well as knowledge, and when I got done what could I present after all, given the rules of the game? I know what my teacher would have done: she would have presented a list of The Four Reasons why American State Capitals are situated in otherwise minor cities, and drilled us till we got them right.

The three methods of heat transfer, as explained in my 1941 textbook called *Modern Physics* (I won't embarass the author by mentioning his name), were as follows:

(a) Conduction,
(b) Convection, and
(c) Radiation.

Without going into details of the molecular theory of matter (and kinetic theory of gases), and the quantum theory of radiation, by which these three words have been analyzed since 1900 or so, let me say that the above list is about as true and illuminating as the following analogy would suggest:

Q. What are the three methods of transfer of bank deposits?
A. 1) Personal check,
2) Cashier's check, and
3) Airmail.

The book could go on to explain that personal checks are generally written in ink while cashier's checks are typed, and guaranteed by the bank. Other useful information might include the speed of airplanes and their tendency to crash from time to time, something not at all true of either sort of check.

Oh, if I were a teacher, what a fine week of the study of finance I could make out of this listing! I swear the analogy is a good one, though I will not otherwise explain the imbecility of the heat transfer listing. Nor will I attempt to trace the historical reasons for the 1941 appearance of precisely that list (It was not invented by the author of my textbook, you may be sure), though there are some.

The question is--as it was with the Properties of Gold, the Causes of the Civil War and the 48 Capital Cities--what did these teachers and textbook writers think they were doing when they arranged for us to gabble these miserable syllables? My own opinion, considered these thirty-odd years, is that they didn't think anything at all. They were doing what they had been told was virtuous and correct, as people do who follow any other ritual.

These lists were not intended to educate any more than a rain dance is intended to bring rain. Everyone gets told that these are the intentions, but (as anthropologists have pointed out in cases like these) to understand the reality one must study the ritual rather than the "belief."

When a workman uses a tool to smooth a piece of wood he doesn't offer prayer, he looks to see whether the wood in fact becomes smooth as a result of his manipulation of that tool. If it doesn't he invents another tool, or uses differently the one he has. Carpentry is not a religion.

The results of ritual are also studied, in a manner of speaking, but not as the carpenter studies the effect of his tools. A successful rain dance verifies the ritual's correctness. An "unsuccessful" rain dance is evidence of sin, or improper incantation, or almost anything except the irrelevance of the ritual to the "intended" result. *Every* result reinforces the faith; it is by this observation that one can recognize--even define--a religion, to distinguish it from what should be the activity of the factory, a government or an educational enterprise.

Just as with rain dances, then, the "educational" process at Central High School had its successes and its failures. I suppose I was among the successes: a solid moral literate productive citizen. The Board of Education had only to point to students like me to prove the efficacy of public education, grades K-12 September through June and attended by the requisite number of certified and licensed teachers and school psychologists. What of the failures? The truants and jail-birds-to-be, the scornful, the drunk, the illiterate? Why, more teachers of course, more psychologists, stiffer licensing laws, Head Start, summer school, Community College. Pray harder, put out more flags.

It is no accident then that the list is the most memorable, because the most characteristic, feature of my school days. A list is a litany, a catechism, a rosary, a chant. Abraham, Isaac, and Jacob; Father, Son and Holy Ghost; Hare Krishna Hare Hare; the Twelve Tribes; the Seven Dwarfs. From Minoan temple to Michigan high school the impulse remains the same.

It will never die, I think. Whatever it is called and whatever the 1st Amendment may say, it is a State religion. In one form or another every State has one. Ours is maybe not as bad as some, but this may not last. Certainly it is getting more expensive all the time.

Relevance

ONCE A young man worked at a desk in the outer office of a Congressman, typing and filing papers. He was a college drop-out, this bright young man, who had been somehow turned off by formal schooling. Not quite a convert to the Counterculture, something in the fever of the times drove him from the classroom to the real world, where men directed other men and the problems of race, poverty and war were on the firing line.

Somehow, then, he got this job, and found it exciting; for the first time he knew what he was doing and why. Never in all his years had he worked so hard, so that in no great time his diligence attracted the personal attention of the Congressman himself.

His lack of education was the pity. The Congressman liked the boy, yet saw that he wrote an ignorant English and knew depressingly little of history, economics or law. What would be his future? Without nurture, his natural ability would go to waste.

So the Congressman took from his own pocket--or from his constituents?--the money to send the young man back to college. Clear up the rough edges, give the boy a background he can build on, Plato, Cicero, McLuhan.

A month later this same Congressman was surprised to find this same young man back at the desk and typewriter. What was he doing there? Explain yourself, young man!

Here is the answer: his college sent him. All students, it was decided by the academic council, must counteract the dead hand of irrelevant classroom exercises by going out into the world. There would be found the education a proper 20th Century college must appreciate as revolutionary and ecstatic. Pursuant to this ideal, our young man had been assigned to the Congressman's office, to perform true and relevant duties and earn a meaningful B.A.

The only difference is that the Congressman now pays the college and not the boy.

Letter From San Francisco --- January 1, 1969

ON TUESDAY afternoon, November 26, 1968, President Robert Smith of the San Francisco State College resigned, and within a few minutes was replaced by a new Acting President, S. I. Hayakawa. Smith himself had been president for less than a year, having replaced John Summerskill, a man whose troubles a year earlier had been very much like Smith's. The beginning of Hayakawa's tenure was greeted by Professor William Stanton of the Economics Department with the sour statement 'He won't last as long as Smith.' One of President Hayakawa's first acts was to notify Stanton that his present contract with San Francisco State will be his last.

The new President, when asked by the press how he hoped to succeed in bringing to an end the strikes and violence which had rendered his campus all but unusable for intellectual purposes since November 6, said he would be 'trying new things.' Over the Thanksgiving weekend holiday he made his plans, and beginning Monday, December 2 the police were out in force, by the hundreds, whereas President Smith had used them only sporadically, never massively, and had on several occasions shut down the campus entirely rather than oppose student violence with enough police power to suppress it.

The first week of Hayakawa's policy was attended by more violence than in all the previous history of San Francisco State. The cry of police brutality brought a number of angry adult non-students onto the campus, among them leaders of the Black and Brown communities of San Francisco, who for a time interposed themselves between police and student strikers, cooling the violence somewhat, but by week's end all was normal again; a number of clubbings and a dozen or so arrests per day. On Friday the 13th, the last day of Hayakawa's second week, he closed the campus a week early for a lengthy Christmas-New Year's holiday. The violence was over for the time being, while all sides (and there were several) are prepared for January 6, when classes are due to open again, and a new phase of the conflict will doubtless surprise everyone who imagines he can predict the outcome.

The student strike was formally declared on November 6, 1968. In the Daily Gator (a student newspaper) of that day, an issue marked STRIKE EDITION, appeared the following article:

BSU explanation of today's strike

The trustees and the administration are preparing to destroy us.

All Black student and Third World student programs and achievements face extermination on this campus.

All Black Studies Department does not exist in reality. It is only on paper as a department. The racists in the administration have been and are destroying the whole concept of Black Studies.

The Trustees are preparing to dissolve the Associated Students, now that the Black and Third World students have developed working programs and brought the college to the community and the community to the college. Tutoring and Special Admissions won't have money to survive on, once the Trustees seize AS funds.

So we must prepare ourselves for a strike. And organize ourselves to take further action.

The Black Student Union and the Black Faculty Union take responsibility for the welfare of all Black people on the campus (workers, students, administrators, faculty).

Therefore we demand the following:

1). That all Black Studies courses being taught through various other departments be immediately part of the Black Studies department and that all the instructors in this department receive full time pay.

2). That Dr. Hare , Chairman of the Black Studies Department, receive a full professorship and a comparable salary according to his qualifications.

3). That there be a Department of Black Studies which will grant a Bachelor's Degree in Black Studies; that the Black Studies Department, chairman, faculty and staff have the sole power to hire faculty and control and determine the destiny of its department.

4). That all unused slots for Black students from Fall 1968 under the Special Admission program be filled in Spring 1969.

5). That all Black students wishing so, be admitted in Fall 1969.

6). That twenty (20) full time teaching positions be allocated to the Department of Black Studies.

7). That Dr. Helen Bedesem be replaced from the position of Financial Aid Officer and that a Black person be hired to direct it, that Third World people have the power to determine how it will be administered.

8). That no disciplinary action will be administered in any way to any students, workers, teachers, or administrators during and after the strike as a consequence of their participation in the strike.

9). That the California State College Trustees not be allowed to dissolve any Black programs on or off San Francisco State College campus.

10). That George Murray maintain his teaching position on campus for 1968-69 academic year.

A second student organization called the Third World Liberation Front, representing Brown Power (Mexican-, Japanese-, Chinese-, and Latin-Americans), put forward in the same paper five Demands of its own:

11). That a School of Ethnic Studies for the ethnic groups involved in the Third World be set up with the students in each particular ethnic organization having the authority and control of the hiring and retention of any faculty member, director, and Administrator, as well as the curriculum in a specific area study;

12). That 50 faculty positions be appropriated to the School of Ethnic Studies, 20 of which would be for the Black Studies program;

13). That, in the Spring semester, the College fulfill its commitment to the non-white students in admitting those that apply;

14). That, in the Fall of 1969, all applications of non-white students be accepted;

15). That George Murray and any other faculty person chosen by non-white people as their teacher be retained in their position.

The SDS (Students for a Democratic Society), a white group which in the past two years had led campus militancy across the country, supported these fifteen Demands, but added none of its own. Throughout the whole affair they have in fact taken a back seat, except on the barricades.

The struggle over the fifteen Demands somewhat resembled a union-management confrontation in industry; this was the flavor given it in the press, and is perhaps the way people outside a University would naturally view it. But it is not the same. When a labor union puts forward a set of demands, they may be unreasonable but they are never merely mad. One can understand a demand for a two dollar an hour pay raise, a counter-offer of fifty cents and a settlement at sixty. The two dollars asked may have been ridiculous, but only as to quantity, not nature. It was a number on a scale which meant something to both sides, a scale within the competence of both sides to discuss, and a scale certainly containing a point at which agreement would ultimately be reached.

The demands at issue at San Francisco State are partly of this nature, but they are very importantly not. For example, a Department of Black Studies must be established immediately, with twenty full-time faculty members. At present there are a few Black Studies courses scattered around various Departments, and perhaps the time equivalent of three full faculty members assigned. The College Faculty had recently, in the normal course of such procedures, been in the process of voting a formal Department into being, while the Administration has been pressing the Trustees to increase its financing. Without the strike the program would have become a Department by September 1969, with three or four full-time professors--and, doubtless, the Professor Hare of Demand No. 2, as Chairman, and within five years the new Department would have grown to some thirty professors. This much was in the works, though it had been hindered this year by a Statewide cutback in college appropriations.

Once the Black Student Union became strident, but well before the real violence on campus, President Smith had already pressed his faculties to give up part of their separate departmental budgets to allow for a Black Studies Faculty of about twelve by January 1969. This involved a fiscal device for which he was still seeking Trustees' approval at the time of his resignation.

Now twenty new positions (Demand No. 6) doesn't seem much in a faculty of seven hundred; the Demand seems quite temperate. But that it should be established immediately, by Presidential fiat, while windows are breaking and fires are being set all around the campus--that was another matter. Academic programs are established and approved by certain faculty committees, after which the President, whose budget is already in arrears, must go to the Trustees, who -----BULLSHIT, cry the strikers, throwing rocks, NOW.

Well, difficult, but perhaps not impossible. Until, of course, you get a good look at the other Demands. Certain technical changes seem to be asked for in the operation of the new Department. It must have a totally Black faculty, not chosen by Deans, Presidents, etc., but by the Department itself--indeed, by its *students,* according to Demand No. 11, from the Third World. While not stated explicitly, the wording of Demands 9, 11, and 15 leave no doubt that the entire program, Black and Brown, is intended for non-white students only. That there will be a sufficiency of such students will be guaranteed by the admission of absolutely all non-white applicants to San Francisco State, whatever their previous academic qualification. The Department (and all Departments of the other Ethnic Studies) will be the creator of its own program, its own degree requirements, without hindrance by the racist pigs, including the Trustees and the other parts of the Faculty. And finally, Associate Professor Hare, now the coordinator of the temporarily scattered Black Studies, must be promoted immediately to full Professor, and be made Chairman of the resulting totally autonomous empire, with its blank check on the State Treasury.

Anyone who has ever been near a University knows how impossible it is for anyone in the whole world to say 'Yes, I grant these demands,' even if he wants to. Power is simply not that centralized. Consider the question of the promotion of Professor Hare. Why not? He is in a responsible position, reputedly a qualified social historian and so on. The fact is that his promotion was already, along with the establishment of his Department, going through the usual faculty-administration procedures. A President cannot override these deliberations, or anticipate their result, without angering his faculty. President Smith, replying to this particular demand, tried hard to indicate that the promotion was really on the way, without of course prejudicing the faculty prerogative to recommend and advise first. Any union negotiator would have known he had that point won already, and would have pushed on to another, but winning real concessions was not the purpose of the Demands. They really were rallying points rather than bargaining points; they were a device to keep the strike in motion, for the Third World students insisted at all times that the package was 'non-negotiable' and had to be granted verbatim before they would permit the campus to be open in peace. Thus 'Why won't the racists promote Dr. Hare?' could be retained for public consumption so long as the other fourteen Demands were not yet met, even though the promotion of Dr. Hare had already been granted to all intents and purposes.

President Smith, in his piteous attempts to negotiate the Demands, could hardly begin to explain how inconsistent it is with his idea of a College, and with the American ideal, to have a racially segregated program and a racial barrier (against whites) in its admission policy. Unlimited Black admissions next fall, given a budget to meet, would mean a quota on whites, after all (Haw, Haw--a budget, he says). Firing the Financial Aid officer out of hand (Demand No. 7), moreover, violates the contract of employment; charges would have to be brought, of incompetence or of racial bias. Due process is not only moral, but is required by the State Administrative Code (Due Process? He should talk; he's never been black).

The demand for educational and administrative autonomy for a Department, even without its segregated composition, would be unprecedented and quite undesirable. The Department would have *more* autonomy (freedom from the Trustees, among other things) than the whole College now has. And what would its degree be worth if it had no standards subject to outside scrutiny? Especially if it began its life flooded with students of inferior preparation, and with a faculty gathered up overnight.

Actually, such an autonomy couldn't be agreed to under existing State law, not only by President Smith but by Chancellor Dumke or Governor Reagan himself. No legislature in all the fifty States would consider making such a thing legal, nor could the Trustees of even a private University do such a thing under its Charter. In short, the proposal is mad, and is the legal equivalent of allowing hospital patients to elect the hospital staff, and to decide the mode of treatment the staff should use.

The medical analogy is in fact fairly close, apart from the Black Separatism feature of the San Francisco State proposal. Hospital patients know less about the subject at stake than the staff does, and yet can claim with as much justice as students that if it is for them that the institution exists. There is another feature in common. Hospitals, like colleges, spend money on research, on the continuing education of their doctors (professors), and on other capital investment whose value to the institution will only appear when the current crop of patients (students) have long been replaced by others. It will always be possible to convince the transients that these long-range expenditures can safely be delayed in favor of something more pressing, like lower fees.

Another group of demands (8, 10, and 15) concerned, as is usual in these affairs, amnesty, especially for George Murray, Minister of Education (no less) of the Black Panther Party. A year ago, Murray led an attack on the offices of the student newspaper, destroying the place and beating up the editor for writing bad editorials. For this he was convicted, later, of assault, and is now out of jail of probation. He was then, and is now, a graduate student in the English Department, and he is now also a part-time instructor in English, where he is said to have some success in teaching poorly-prepared college freshmen to read, in the remedial program associated with the Special Admissions the strikers now want expanded to include all comers.

Smith, on becoming President, not only pardoned Murray for his assaults and vandalism, but promised to expand ghetto admissions and promised a number of other black-oriented educational goodies which cost money he could only hope, at the time, to get from the Trustees. He did all a man could do in that direction, and enjoyed a surprisingly wide popularity with the faculty and students. But it was Murray, or the Murray question, which came back to finish President Smith's regime.

Towards the end of October, before the strike began but when the demands of the Black Student Union were growing heated, George Murray spoke on campus, warning his followers that they should bring guns with themselves when they came to school, to protect themselves from the pigs the racist imperialist administration would be soon resorting to in order to thwart the just demands of the Third World. This speech among others so angered Glen Dumke, Smith's immediate superior in the State College system, that Dumke publicly ordered Smith to suspend Murray.

Smith had already been treading an impossible tightrope, trying to pacify the Black militants by promising speed on the expansion of Black Studies and the admission of Black students while trying to make those promises good by appealing to Dumke and the Trustees for money they quite knowingly hadn't given him for these purposes. Smith resisted carrying out the suspension order for twenty-four hours, during which time he tried sending telegrams and telephoning to Chancellor Dumke, pleading for a meeting. If Murray's speech were an offense sufficient for suspension or expulsion, the College had its own disciplinary procedures, after all, and Smith had already set these in motion. But Dumke needed no such explanation and had no conference with Smith, who then obeyed the order as gently as he could, suspending Murray without prejudice for one month at full pay while the campus courts were being convened to hear his case more formally. It did not help; a week later the strike was on. The Demand concerning Murray was a escalation of 'status quo ante'; it was nothing less than a full pardon for anything Murray, or any other person acting in the name of the strike, had done or would do between last year and whenever all fifteen Demands were finally granted.

If the fifteen Demands only partly resemble the sort of thing a labor union asks for, a student strike, similarly, only partly resembles an industrial strike. By not going to class, students are not, after all, withholding any essential service from the College. They parade around with placards, and if it goes on long enough they flunk their courses. At least, this is all one could expect of a strike in its pure form, so long as the strikers are, as they were at San Francisco State, a small minority of the student body, the rest of whom go to their classes. At Berkeley across the bay, at about the same time, a strike was called over a rather complicated question concerning another Black Panther, Eldridge Cleaver, but it collapsed after one day from lack of general interest among the students, and no support whatever among the faculty. The Blacks at State did not let this happen.

During the first few days, when almost all classes were meeting, small groups of strikers, usually pairs, went around visiting all classes they could, interrupting them with loud exhortations to come join the strike. Sometimes they were polite, asked permission from the instructor to explain the strike issues to the class, did so, and departed. Others, not so polite, set fires in washrooms, assaulted students who angered them, and carried on generally disruptive behavior. President Smith had a number of plainclothes police on campus trying to keep order quietly; he was still attempting to preserve the sentimental tradition of 'no police on campus,' or at least its appearance. However, the elite riot police of San Francisco, called the Tac Squad, was quartered nearby; they made their first appearance when the strike was about a week old. That day it was clear that order could not be preserved on the cheap, and Smith closed the campus for a breather. But the breather got him nowhere; Faculty meetings, Senate meetings, appeals to the strikers for negotiations--nothing made any difference. The fifteen Demands were non-negotiable, and the College must remain shut until they were met.

The next opening of the campus lasted two days, days during which very little education went on. Nobody could keep track of which professors were or were not meeting their classes. Some professors openly supported the strike, and picketed, though they did not set any fires or throw rocks. Other professors said the campus was too dangerous for class, and either did not meet them or held them off campus in their homes or in nearby churches or so. Who could say whether they were on strike? And of course lots of students stayed home even if their classes met. More fires, more assaults, more police, and on Friday, November 22, Smith closed it up officially again.

This time Chancellor Dumke and the Trustees (and it should be remembered that Governor Reagan and Superintendent of Instruction Max Rafferty were Trustees by virtue of their offices) had enough of temporizing; they ordered Smith to open the campus Monday, and to keep it open. Smith acceded, formally, but tried one more gambit of foredoomed conciliation. He announced that the campus would be open the following week, actually the three days of November 25-27, since Thursday would be Thanksgiving Day and school was in any case out for the long weekend, but he also announced that the academic program for those three days would be replaced by another sort of educational experience; a great Convocation in the large Auditorium for purposes of permitting all sides of the current difficulty to explain their views. By closed circuit TV the proceedings would be seen in all parts of the campus, for those who could not fit into the auditorium. Everyone could explain his case in an atmosphere free of suspicion and recrimination, and in the best tradition of the Academy the truth would surely be arrived at, and as surely agreed to by those who had earlier walked in darknes.

To get the strikers to agree to participate in the Convocation took all weekend. They were finally persuaded that the campus was really closed, and that the discussions would be for information only, since negotiation or an open campus were out of the question. The Trustees had dispersed since their order for an open campus was given, but presumably Smith hoped to be able to convince them after the fact that he had indeed kept the campus open, just as he had convinced the

Blacks that it was closed. The local Educational TV station was going to cover the proceedings in full, and participatory democracy, on public display, was to produce Smith's miracle.

It did not come off. Monday's opening session was held up for four hours over a procedural wrangle before it even began. That dispute was settled by an agreement that the fifteen Demands were to be considered as a unit, instead of separately, whatever that might mean. What it meant to the Third World militants, apparently, was that the discussion should be a series of generalized diatribes (which had to be heard to be believed). On TV a delay circuit was used, permitting erasure of the shorter words, though on the radio station which carried it everything came through. There were standard rally exhortations, condemnations of the racist College, of Pig Dumke and so on, warnings of blood in the streets and the inevitable takeover of white America by those (Blacks) who had built the nation but had the fruits of their labor stolen. The death of capitalism was announced, and of the white imperialist occupation of the Black communities (In Black Panther nomenclature, Stokeley Carmichel is already Prime Minister of Colonized Afro-America). And of course every speech breathed intransigence on every detail of the fifteen Demands.

A few speakers, on the second day, notably among the Chinese and Mexican students, addressed themselves more reasonably to the problem of their communities, and spoke touchingly of their dream of the contribution San Francisco State College might make to the study and preservation of their cultures in America, and the alleviation of their poverty, ignorance and indignity. Such talk, however, was infrequent: most was blatant diatribe and insult, designed to make agreement a ludicrous notion. One felt sorry for those Third World students who were persuaded they were doing their people some good by joining a united front led by cynics who had no intention of gaining anything that day but anger, police confrontation and anarchy.

The Administration and 'conservative' faculty speakers, including Smith and the Chairman of the Faculty Senate, were practically tongue-tied in reply. Having been blasted as Pigs, Nazis, Mother-Fuckers, theives and murderers of 400 years' standing, liars, cheats, racists and Klansmen, having been charged with a 400-year rape of Black culture, dignity, wealth, and women, it was a bit difficult to explain that the promotion of Associate Professor Hare was a matter for study by the senior faculty of his present Department. . . .

The Black Panther Party Platform of 1966, an official document, contains, among others, the following statements:

"We want all black men to be exempt from military service. . . Black people should not be forced to fight in the military service to defend a racist government that does not protect us. . .

"We want freedom for all black men held in federal, state, county and city prisons and jails. . . because they have not received a fair and impartial trial.

"We want. . .a United Nations-supervised plebiscite to be held throughout the black colony in which only black colonial subjects will be allowed to participate, for the purpose of determining the will of black people as to their national destiny."

The demand for a plebiscite is followed by a lengthy quotation from the Declaration of Independence, justifying the demand for Black independence as analogous to that of the Thirteen Colonies. It is necessary to understand that the Black Student Unions in our colleges, particularly at San Francisco State, subscribe to these doctrines, in order to understand how they can arrive at 'educational' demands so foreign to the thinking of traditional academics and administrators. The demand for total autonomy of the Black Studies Department, plainly impossible in today's College context, becomes quite reasonable to a youth who seriously looks forward to a Black Nation within America. He challenges the authority of the State of California to tell him anything at all, neither what he shall learn, nor who shall teach him. The State has stolen his people's wealth; with this money it will jolly well pay a few professors of the sort he chooses--and that will be only the beginning of the repayment.

The unsophisticated striker, then, was merely furious that people like Smith could not understand the justice, nay, the necessity, of such demands. The leaders, more sophisticated, understood well that Smith could not possible accede. That was just as well, indeed, better, for the resulting strife would generate a deeper anger in the as yet undecided.

Smith attended Monday's convocation; Tuesday he was summoned to a hastily convened meeting of the Trustees. Clearly he was on the carpet. Either he would return with some startling concession (from Reagan?), or he would be fired, or he would resign. Back at the auditorium the talking went on and on. Towards 4:00 p.m.

the Third World left the stage and had a caucus, and then Professor Hare returned to the platform and interrupted a particularly bumbling faculty speaker to make an announcement. I am not sure exactly who was on the stage at the time, as I was listening to the radio, taping the proceedings, but there were at least the Chairman of the meeting and two other professors or administrators (who will be identified as Professors A and B in what follows), Professor Hare, and, for the Third World Students, their most articulate spokesman, Roger Alvarado.

Professor Hare: I have an announcement. The Third World and Black Students have come to a painful conclusion, after a good deal of deliberation and extending themselves in trying to be tolerant of all the rhetoric and dialogue and empty promises, so that we feel that it is time for people to indicate where they stand, and what they are going to do, if anything. So therefore we are calling for a vote of the faculty on this matter: whether they will meet the Demands, whether they favor or support the meeting of the Demands, by 2:00 o'clock tomorrow, and the students--we are announcing this at this time because we feel that we are aware of the fact that it takes time to organize--to get your own things together, and so that you can have time to do that, we would like to give you the time to start at this particular moment, right now, to decide and organize yourselves for casting a vote on tomorrow at 2 o'clock.

Meanwhile, at 9:30 tomorrow morning we will assemble here, and we are asking all the students to come out tomorrow morning because we are going to ask there for the students to vote and to indicate their position. Thank you.

Chairman: This of course is a change in the format of the Convocation [laughter, from the audience], but I assume this would be discussed by the Planning Committee, which has been in charge of, you know, how we proceed. We could not make a decision *here* on that.

Professor Hare: The Committee on the Dialogue has decided--at least the Black Student part of it, and the Third World Student part of it, and the faculty (Black and Third World) part of it--that this is the way it will go. And what you decide will not affect the decision of these persons. Tomorrow the Faculty will vote at 2:00, and in the morning at the Convocation we will have facilities so that the students can vote tomorrow morning.

Professor A: Mr. Chairman, I have certainly received the request from Dr. Nathan Hare, and will carry this to the Faculty. Naturally, I can't commit the Faculty at this time.

[a few seconds of puzzled silence ensues, with murmurs from the audience, which, late on the second day, has been much reduced from the earlier full house, and consists mainly of strike supporters]

Professor B: Mr. Chairman, I presume we are still discussing the Second Demand.

Chairman: No, I think we are not, right now [delighted laughter from the audience]. Right now there's been some suggestion of a change in the plan of the program, and I am not sure I understand it; I want to make very clear about it. Do I understand that the Third World, including the Black Student Union, have decided not to go on with the Convocation as it has been planned by the Planning Committee of the Convocation? Is that what I understand? Is that clear?

Professor Hare: I don't want to get into a dialogue on the announcement. Ya wanna have a Convocation on that, too? Let's have a Convocation on the Announcement, and explain it well. I think it's pretty clear. You want me to indicate it again--

Chairman: Well, wait a minute--

Professor Hare: ---The Faculty will vote tomorrow at 2:00; the students will vote tomorrow morning at the 9:30 assembly, uh, Convocation. Now, if you want to have a convocation on the announcement, then indicate so by a voice vote at this time.

Professor A: Mr. Hare, the Faculty *may* vote, not *shall* vote.

Professor B: Mr. Hare, are you calling for a general student body vote, is that it? [laughter at the nonplussed faculty on stage]

Chairman: Well, let me just say, from my point of view: The Committee--my boss, the Committee who are planning this conference,. . .

Well, so it went for a few minutes. The vote called for would be participatory democracy at its best; who knows where most of the faculty and students were, at that time? Out of town for the Thanksgiving weekend, most likely, or at best not listening to the radio at the time. There was no question how the few hundred in the auditorium would vote. In the audience, while those on stage were trying to figure out something useful to do or say, a man stood up and began what turned out to be a full ten-minute speech. He was Harry James Tate, Jr., he said, representing the Poor People's Crusade in San

Francisco. He spoke with the fervor and authority of a gospel preacher, damning the College administration all the way up to the Governor, and he produced the first real enthusiasm of the Convocation. At the end of it the audience was chanting Strike, Strike, Strike!

Chairman: Sounds like it's possible that we might be able to learn something from our students [cheers]. We have about fifteen minutes left now[Tate, from the audience: You got all the time in the world, man!]. Roger? Roger Alvarado would like to say something.

[Roger Alvarado is the principal spokesman for the striking Third World students, apart from the blacks.]

Alvarado: I picked up this piece of information today, which was sent to a student by the Administration, signed by the Dean of Students. It reads, 'You are hereby notified that as a result of your activity on campus of November 13, 1968, which resulted in your arrest by the San Francisco Police Department, College disciplinary action is being taken against you pursuant to Section 4131 Title 5 of the California Administrative Code, a copy of which is attached. You will be required to appear before a College Disciplinary Hearing Panel. As a result of this disciplinary hearing, you will [this is the word Alvarado used, though it seems doubtful the letter could have prejudged the outcome] be placed on probation, suspended or expelled from the College. You will be notified of the exact time of the hearing. It will be scheduled as soon as possible.'

You see, you see--again--again--we have gone down, we have listened to the man, stupidly--I have to admit it--like--a pack of fools, like a pack of fools.

We got out asses up here, we agreed to talk, we agreed to say what we had to say--again--we had a commitment from Smith. Smith didn't have enough respect to come here, and relate to Third World People, today. Instead, he's gonna listen to the politicians, and the Board of Trustees tell him what to do, and when he *knows* what's going on here at this campus, and he *knows* the people want to hear where he's at--he's gonna go down and talk to the man!

At the same time, he's gonna come down, and out front--out front--think he's gonna get away with going against--directly against--one of the demands that we stipulated. One of the Demands says, and it says it very clearly: Nobody--Nobody!--will be affected in any way by this College for their activities in the strike. It says it very clearly.

What the man has done now is that he comes down with this thing--quietly--he just mails it away, expects somebody to go ahead and take it for nothing! Go ahead and take it lying down. Well I say no! I say no! I say we have to deal with it, I say we have to deal with it together as a *people* here. Otherwise we don't have a damn thing at all. We don't have a damn thing at all! Let's put it where it belongs!

We are talking basically about directing the course of our education. What we are saying tomorrow is that we want you to vote as to where you are in that. If you can recognize that, if you can recognize the legitimacy of our demands, the validity of our demands and the position, and the position of us as Third World people on this Campus and our people's needs in this city and this country and around this world--

Then, let's put it where it belongs! If we're gonna have to hand it to Smith, then we put it to Smith. If we have to hand it to Dumke, then we hand it to Dumke. If we have to hand it to the Board of Trustees, let's put it where we have to put it!

But this bickering, and this getting put up here on front, and on gan--because you can't even listen, you can't even *listen* to the son of a bitch 'cause he's gonna lie to you anyway! He's gonna lie to you anyway! He's gonna cheat you, he's gonna make you look like a fool, because you're concerned.

The Brothers of the Third World, when they heard about the Convocation--and *we blew,* we blew harder than we blew the first time! We got the Brothers to go along with us. It took us--all night, but we did it. We come walking back in here, and this is what we get, as a reaction. As a reaction!

You can't--there is no person on this College; I don't see, I don't understand how anybody on this college could think, in any way, that President Smith or any one of the Administrators up there in that building: Don Garrity, Fern Goodell, or Glenn Smith, any one of them, four--I don't see how anybody on this campus could think that they could trust them. Could even *imagine* they could trust them.

'Cause they have done it to us, they have done it *again* to us! They call on the pigs rather than deal with the Demands. We try to educate people as to what the Demands are, and they are still sending our people to the pigs. We have got no other alternative. This school is closed. And it stays closed [cheers]. If Smith is gonna stand in the middle, then let him stand in the middle. We're gonna go ahead and take care of Dumke, 'cause that's where it's at now. We're gonna go talk to Dumke. We're gonna tell him what we want, and then we're gonna listen to him. Bullshit!

Tomorrow, as you heard Dr. Hare explain, we are calling for a vote of the people. A vote of the people. We are ready to take power, and we will take it all the way. At 9:30 we have asked the students of this College to be here and to make their position clear. At 2:00 tomorrow afternoon, we have asked the Faculty to come here and make *their* position clear. The question is simple: Do you support the fifteen Demands of the BSU and Third World Liberation Front--to go on strike?

The Convocation is over.

[here the Third World students and faculty, on stage and in the audience, left the hall]

The Chairman of the no longer existent Convocation announced, for the microphone I suppose, that professors ought to come to campus the next day, as some meetings might be held, and he asked for an immediate meeting of the Convocation organizers. It didn't matter. Within the hour the announcement of Smith's resignation was in the newspapers, and the appointment of Hayakawa. Smith had indeed been down talking to the man.

Hayakawa's first act was to declare the campus closed on Wednesday. The press described this as a cancellation of the rest of Smith's Convocation; they could not have been listening to Hare and Alvarado that day. The niceties of the Wednesday vote, which had everybody but its proponents so puzzled, thus turned moot. On Sunday Hayakawa announced that the campus would reopen Monday, that sound trucks and rallies on campus were forbidden during a Period of Emergency of indefinite duration, and that whatever police protection might be needed would be provided. On the other hand, he was anxious to meet with any and all persons who had a grievance; only there was no reason he could see for stopping education, for those who wanted it, while the negotiations proceeded. He reminded professors that State law provided that persons who willfully failed to meet their instructional obligations for five days without valid reason were automatically regarded as having resigned. Governor Reagan said, 'I think we've found our man.'

I don't have a tape of Monday's rally and riot, but I do have extensive tapes of those of Tuesday and Thursday, which were similar. These reports were broadcast by KPFA, a Berkeley listener-supported radio station, exactly as they were recorded *in situ* by their own reporter. In the middle of the College campus there is a green, facing the library, the Student Union and a couple of other buildings. To one side of the green is the Free Speech Platform, which was dedicated seven years ago with considerable ceremony, celebrating a victory whose details I don't know over men of little soul. It is used incessantly, generally at noontime, for free speech.

On Tuesday, December 3, the second day of the post-Smith, or Hayakawa phase of the strike, classes were being held all over campus. During the morning, as during the preceding day, there had been riots, bloodied heads, arrests. Hayakawa's order forbidding rallies had been ignored on Monday, and was being ignored on Tuesday as well. The second-last speaker, a white student, concluded his remarks with:

'...the ruling class of this state has shown its bankruptcy. I don't think we have to worry about them, about pleasing or displeasing, about saying 'pretty please' to them. I think we're through with that on this campus, and I think we're going to be through with that in this country and on other campuses around the country. We're gonna continue to fight, continue to struggle, and struggle and fight until we win.'

The crowd of somewhere between one and three thousand applauded temperately. Then a Black student spoke:

'All right. You remember that nine students or more have been arrested, have been suspended, and still more students are goin' to be suspended! You know what has to be done. Everyone knows what has to be done, now. Who's goan move? Who's goan move? WHO'S GOAN MOVE?

'. . . The Tac Squad is over there, and back here, and National Guardsmen's on their way. . .Shut it down! Shut the school down! Shut it down! Let's move to BSS right now.'

BSS is *Business and Social Science,* the name of one of the larger buildings on campus. There followed a brief discussion near the platform as to whether the crowd should break into several groups, attacking different buildings, or stay together. A democratic decision was arrived at, to go in one group to BSS. About one-third of the crowd did so, the rest standing back, ringing the green, watching, along with the reporter. The moving mob chanted 'On strike; shut it down!, in a rhythm reminiscent of the French chant 'Algérie. . .Françaises!' of the revolution which brought De Gaulle to power, instead of securing Algeria for France.

The Tactical Squad stayed for a time on the library steps, and other San Francisco police, augmented by detachments from nearby towns, did nothing at first. There were also police inside the buildings, so the crowd did not enter BSS, but pounded on the front door and on pots and pans some carried with them as noisemakers. Then rocks were thrown at windows. Lots of windows broken, said the reporter. Tac Squad moves in formation towards the group, people scattering, but only onlookers. Police moving slowly. On Strike, Shut It Down. Police moving up from another direction. The police near BSS now being pelted with rocks, thrown from the onlooker crowd as much as from the besiegers of BSS. One policeman hit by a rock. Now they're wading into the crowd and grabbing people. Everybody is being ordered (bullhorn) to disperse, but nobody dispersing. The police are surrounded now, by a loose-weaving mob. From time to time a cop rushes into the crowd and grabs someone, hits him with a stick, drags him back to the police area, pins him to the ground. The police are acting very defensive, the reporter says, constantly returning to the protection of their formation. They are being pushed into a tighter circle. They form ranks. There's a black with a bloody head. There the police are beating a kid who was already on the ground, and the Tac Squad is slowly pushing people back. Two thousand people around about fifty policemen. There a cameraman was hit by a rock from the crowd, from the surrounding innocent bystanders. And the reporter, who was, by the way, a partisan of the strike, reported: 'There is a big silence now. A shocked look on everybody's face.'

Well, it goes on like that, until the crowd finally was dispersed. That Tuesday was the worst day of the whole strike so far, for violence and arrests; some forty-five were arrested, and according to the principals a good number of those arrested were beaten up severely in the paddy wagons, after arrest.

On the following day, December 4, the noon rally, still illegal by Hayakawa's earlier proclamation, but still left alone by the police, was addressed by Hank McGuckin, a San Francisco State professor:

"I want to speak for one minute as a professor of speech, about free assembly and free speech, and regulations which would prohibit what we're doing here today. . . ."

He reminded the audience that he had been among those who had dedicated the Free Speech Platform seven years earlier, and he quoted some fearless words from that earlier speech of his in defense of free speech. He stood by those words, he said. He went on,

"Regulations which prohibit free expression and assembly on a campus make all my degrees, make all my teaching, make my department, make my discipline, make my existence as a man--meaningless, and I'm not gonna give them up. . . .If this be insubordination, make the most of it.!"

Professor McGuckin was followed by Jerry Varnado, Coordinator of the Black Students' Union, who wasted no time defending free speech. He is a student, not a professor, and had no seven-year-old notes to quote from.

Varnado: "It is the position of the Black Student Union, the Central Committee, of passage by the people, it says: The seizure of power by armed struggle, by armed struggle, the settlement of the issue by war, and the highest form of revolution, --- we got to rip-off the slave-master, we got to! We got to!"

And with this the crowd moved to the Administration Building shouting 'Hayakawa!' and later developing the rhythmic chant 'We want the puppet' 'We want the puppet'. (The acting President had been characterized, from the moment of his appointment, as a puppet for the trustees.) The mob did invade the Administration Building, pounding on Hayakawa's door and chanting, while Hayakawa's voice came out of the outdoor loudspeakers informing the mob that they must disperse. Finally, when free speech grew so vehement that Hayakawa's door was in danger of being broken down, one of the pigs in the building drew his gun and pointed it at the ceiling. Within a few minutes the building was empty, and the scene from then on resembled that of the preceding day. Broken windows, rocks thrown at the police, and finally, the inevitable unprovoked police brutality was unleashed on the unsuspecting group of free speakers.

The rioting of those first three days not only 'radicalized' a good number of innocent students (innocent of thought and reflection, I mean, and curiously shocked when the same impulse which sends others to football rallies and bonfires sends them to celebrations which end in their being clubbed and jailed), it enlarged the corps of free speakers available to go around the city of San Francisco carrying the message to the public. Community meetings were organized in the non-white neighborhoods, and a good number of ministers, the editor of a Negro newspaper, a Negro State Assemblyman, a Negro City Councilman and others assisted the efforts of the students. Leaflets covered the city, passed out in front of the department stores and groceries. 'Liberal' voices were heard on the radio and television, and in the newspapers, protesting the brutality of the police, while the Mayor and Hayakawa tried to explain that riot is not always a creation of the police.

On Thursday, December 5, the noon rally was no longer a student-faculty affair. Two busloads of non-white community leaders came to the free speech platform and endorsed the fifteen Demands, and they paid special attention to the police. One or two of them were arrested in the rather mild riot which followed; they were arrested for failure to disperse, and fomenting riot and so on, but that day there was little violence, due entirely to the presence of the notables, who regarded themselves as a physical barrier between the idealistic students and the revenging cops. They warned the police, on television, that arrests were the police function, not punishment of malefactors. In this, of course, they were quite right. And in principle, when a man assaults me, I am not entitled to hit him back either; I should bring my complaint to court. Just the same, one does not have to defend the police to remark what a useful red herring the cry of Cossack is. And for a professor, under the circumstances, to go yammering about free speech is only more evidence that professors can be as mendacious as the next men.

Yet such words have their effect away from the Free Speech platform. The subtleties of the fifteen Demands, their history and the details of their promulgation and non-negotiation, are naturally unknown to most of the public. That Hayakawa has been entirely unable to induce a single representative of the BSU or Third World students to talk to him, or even so much as acknowledge his existence, face to face, is not something which the newspapers think worth mentioning every day. One gets, in casual reading, a vague picture of struggle, and one interprets the right and wrong of the matter according to his previous experience or prejudice.

One evening, it was Wednesday, December 5, I was driving from

Berkeley to San Francisco and stopped in a gas station. The attendant was black, perhaps thirty years old. I stayed in my seat listening to the radio, which was reporting the riot of the day, and I asked him what he thought of it all. He gave me his view with vigor. Two of his neighbors, he said, were San Francisco State students, and it was 'bout time the kids were given some say around that place'. Since I am white, and a customer, I think he omitted part of what he thought, which was that the police being on Hayakawa's side meant that the strikers could be no other than justified in whatever they did.

The 'moderate' sentiment, often voiced in the press or radio, despite the militants' reiterated characterization of the media as counter-revolutionary and racist, often goes something like this: "Sure, the kids shouldn't throw rocks, but only a few do, after all. Is that a reason to beat them up by the hundreds? And why don't they listen to what the kids are trying to say? What's Hayakawa *doing,* besides putting cops all around? Is that a way to run a school? Cops have no place on a campus, after all; you can't teach anyone anything at the point of a gun."

True enough, but the lesson is that nobody is in fact learning anything academic at State these days. To think the lesson is that the police should forthwith be moved off campus, so learning can proceed, is a mistake. This was in fact tried. At another college nearby, in San Mateo--this is a junior, two-year, college, but run by the State-the BSU was engaged in a dispute with the administration over issues similar to those at San Francisco State when the BSU decided to have a big rally of such a nature that it was feared that violence would really become serious. The president, and this was about December 15, after conferring with the student leaders, decided to permit the rally and keep all police, overt and covert, off the campus. Thus he did in fact avoid a police riot. All he got was a pure student riot, without police brutality, but with seven persons beaten up by iron pipes so that they had to go to the hospital, and with damage to his campus of about fifty thousand dollars. Of course the police did arrive after a while, and the campus has been an armed camp ever since. And now the black leaders, since the details of that day are pretty far in the background, are talking about the presence of police at San Mateo as if it were an invention of the President's designed to generate a student revolt.

So it is in San Francisco. At least half the militants' rhetoric suggests that the troubles are because of the police, though some professors continue to cite denial of free speech. It sounds as if the only Demand in question is the demand that the campus be shut down; once Hayakawa shuts down the campus, they will be willing to talk, but not to Hayakawa. They will talk only to the Trustees, and only about the manner of implementation of their demands, the acceptance of which is of course a precondition. In this they are being a good deal less flexible than, for example, Ho Chi Minh, one of their heros.

So riot was the order of the day, day after day, until Friday, December 13, when Hayakawa did in fact close the campus a week early for the Christmas holiday. Meanwhile, Hayakawa and the Faculty Senate composed a detailed answer to the Demands, stating which could be met, which could not, and which had to wait for State funds.

The Black Studies Department, with Hare as Chairman, is being put through, beginning with the February semester. Money has been found for some twelve professors, as a start. The Ethnic Studies School will be set up, and its detailed planning is going forward, so far as faculty committee can do that without participation of those who have been asking for it. The Student Aid officer will henceforward be given an 'assistant', a Black, who will have sole jurisdiction over aid to Third World students. But that's about all. No amnesty; the usual campus disciplinary boards will operate, for Murray as well as for the others. No total autonomy; the new Departments will have structures equivalent to those of the old. No unlimited admission of non-whites, though certain unfilled quotas will be filled with sub-qualified students in February, and an expansion of the program will be sought from the Trustees (ultimately, since this takes money, from the Legislature).

But these announcements have been made into a void; nobody is listening. Other attempts are being made. San Francisco's Mayor Alioto, well known for his success at settling labor disputes, has appointed a Citizens' Committee, which is busy talking to representatives of the American Federation of Teachers and respresentatives of the Trustees. The AFT has over three hundred members among the San Francisco State faculty, and has taken a stand supporting the fifteen Demands. It has sweetened the kitty somewhat by adding some demands of its own concerning wages and working conditions (necessary because the national union, and other unions, might look dimly on a purely political strike), and is threatening a strike of its own on January 6, when school is supposed to reopen. The AFT represents only a minority of the faculty, and not all of these are necessarily anxious to strike.

The California State Employees' Association, a sort of rival union which has many more members, also non-academic membership, has called the AFT threat irresponsible, and will not honor any picket lines the AFT may set up. Probably no other union will either, since the AFT has no contract with San Francisco State, and no recognition; in other words it is not part of the standard union structure. Still, high-powered out-of-state mediators are working on this phase of the dispute, but the issues are so confused that nobody really has the authority to address himself to the whole range of issues. Roger Alvarado is reported in the newspapers as being 'pessimistic' about the possibility of settlement along this front. Since that is like Nasser being pessimistic about an end to the middle east state-of-war, it must be taken as authoritative.

Other Citizens' Committees have set themselves up, and 'Silent Majority' groups, but it is really futile to go into the mare's nest of negotiation. The fundamental fact is that the rock-throwing students are not a party to any negotiation at all. They in fact are busy extending the conflict. Every high school in San Francisco, or in the whole bay area, which has a Black Students Union, is under threat of a strike, or worse. There are local issues in each, being worked up for publication, and there is sympathy for the brothers at San Francisco State. Similarly in all the other Colleges of the State College System. The week of January 6 will see massive demonstrations at San Francisco State such as have not been seen before, because the call is out all over the state for students to come down all week and aid in the free speech. And the published aim of the BSU is to close down the whole state system.

The revolution is no longer, if it ever was, a fight for equality of opportunity, or free speech, or relevant education; it is now simply an attack from the ghetto on a peculiarly vulnerable institution of the State. It is a generalized attack, without any more goal than the riots of Watts and Detroit, but it has the advantage that what is being destroyed is not the corner grocery, or the apartment one lives in, but a thing precious only to the bourgeois oppressor.

Meanwhile, what is the Faculty doing? Except for the militants, who are really very few, they have folded up. Faculties are incapable, I think, of speaking clearly about anything. The AFT, by holding out the prospect of economic gain, may get more support than would ordinarily go to the student strikers; I know one AFT member who, rather than argue the morality or justice of the cause, says he will walk out with his union if it gets the approval of the parent labor council. For this he may lose his job, but it saves having to take a real stand. This same man, typical of many, did not support the student strike overtly, but also did not hold classes on campus; he held his classes in his home, for whoever could get there, in the evenings. Too dangerous on campus; his excuse is clear. He is not yet on strike, but he is giving Hayakawa no comfort either. And he has the heady moral pleasure of being true to his profession. Not many students have been coming to his classes, but c'est la guerre. What sort of grades will he give the missing students when the end of the semester rolls around? All Bs, he figures. Why make trouble?

But the Faculty has made no public utterance either in favor of the strikers or against it. It does a lot of muttering here and there. You see them on TV programs deploring the Trustees' interference with campus autonomy. They hate Reagan for many reasons, they regret the failure of a bond proposal at the last election, they point to the lack of educational opportunity among the poor, they complain that Hayakawa was appointed without approval of their Committee on Presidential Appointment, and they talk a lot about due process in connection with Murray.

But if 'interference with campus autonomy' is an issue, what about the interference which began it all: the interference of a black community which demands college degrees for its children, preferential admissions, and a novel curriculum (which the Faculty certainly never thought to institute out of its own wisdom) glorifying black culture and history. The professorial doublethink is willing to regard the voice of the ghetto, or of its self-appointed spokesmen, as a legitimate voice in the College, but contemns the voice of the elected Legislature and Governor, even the voice of its own College Administration, as illegitimate interference.

Professors are fond of saying, in most colleges I have seen, that the faculty *is* the College. Students are apprentices, perhaps customers, being led along the path of truth by the faculty, while the Administration is a cadre of errand boys who keep the buildings in order and see to it that the retirement fund doesn't get lost. Trustees? They aren't even part of the College; they should watch the money and make it grow, and then pass it out without murmur when the faculty sees educational need and votes the necessary request.

This romantic view has no basis in the history of American colleges. Colleges were at first servants of the churches which established them. Later, when the State Universities were being set up, most of them became, or were created as, servants of the State. It was no hunger for more Truth on the part of the existing faculties in 1850 which caused the initiation of the great state schools of agriculture and forestry. Later, in response to another extramural need, schools of engineering sprang up everywhere, and of education, and of business administration. How did all this happen? Did the faculties of classics and theology rise up demanding relevance in education? Not a bit. The State legislatures saw the need, paid the money and got the product. Private universities were a little slower, but private philanthropy's interests were not that much different; Harvard and Chicago got their engineering schools too.

And then, then, the faculty of philosophy was able to decide in solemn gowned conclave that the study of agriculture and engineering could be made to be exciting intellectual challenges, quite the equivalent of Latin in their value to the untrammelled human spirit. The rhetoric of free, courageous enquiry has now penetrated the speeches of Deans of Business Administration, men willing to attack a dangerous accounting problem with all the serenity of Socrates, though they be hanged for it.

The history of faculty independence and courage has its moments. The names of Thorstein Veblen and Bertrand Russell come to mind; they had courage. But they only dramatize their own rarety. They violated rules (sexual, mainly) held so dear by their courageous colleagues that they were booted out at the first whiff of unfortunate publicity reflecting unfavorably on the dignity of the profession. In 1917 the colleges suddenly stopped teaching German, for fear the patriotic citizens and students would burn down the Modern Languages Building, or cut off funds from the Legislature.

Until 1946 a Jew could hardly find a professorial job anywhere. I have seen an old telegram of recommendation, dated 1937, in the files of a mathematics department known to me. In the fifteen or so words his budget allowed, the professor recommending the young man managed to include the words NOT JEWISH DESPITE NAME.

In 1952, when I first became a professor, fear of McCarthy and the Congressional Committees was abroad, and it was fully shared by the academics. Many a learned faculty debate was held that year--I attended one of them--at which freedom of enquiry and speech was defended against all comers, except for genuine Communists. These, it was argued, had a 'prior commitment to a certain version of truth' and therefore were not entitled to teaching positions, which should be reserved to the free. This was said in all seriousness! How curious it is that precisely in 1952 it should have been precisely that brand of prior commitment which was disqualified by the assembled seekers for truth, whose counterparts today are exalting 'commitment' as more precious than rubies, or knowledge. Among the 1952 Seekers were of course professors of football, of audiovisual technique, of secondary school administration, whose prior commitment to Christian Science or astrology would of course never be mentioned by anyone with an ounce of decency.

Now in 1966-1968 the faculties are folding up once again under pressure from a new front. The enemy now is the public, but not the same public which through its legislatures a century ago introduced agriculture and engineering, and has built great research libraries and cyclotrons. It is a local public, the public which (but for its color) burns crosses on lawns. The professors have fallen for Participatory Democracy, not because they favor it but because, like the McCarthy of 1952, it is making the most noise near their classrooms.

Through sheer good luck, the rising wealth of the nation and the interplay of social and technological forces, the academic profession has become blessed in this generation with more freedom to pursue the ends of education, and to influence the rising generation, then it has ever enjoyed in the history of the world. The prestige (and economic value) of research has permitted them to devote more of their time, with rising salaries, to their own interests than ever. A steeply rising population, and per capita wealth, has pushed college enrollments up faster than professors can be found for them, so that all guild barriers to entrance to the profession have fallen. Negroes, Jews, pot-smokers, atheists, free-love advocates--all can be professors now, if they know their subject. Nothing short of prison can drive them from the ranks.

It is a dream come true, for which the professors take full credit even as they take full advantage of it. On the Trustees' payroll, they can spit in the Trustees' eye, in both State and private institutions. No City Hall or Legislature can push *them* around; quite the reverse, since their services are so much sought. Economists, statisticians, sociologists, educators, even historians and linguists. And the City Hall is decorated with their art, and the Inaugurations are graced with their poetry and music. Ay, until two or three years ago it seemed we were on our way to becoming a kingdom of philosophers, beyond the dream of Plato.

Well, the profession is too busy patting itself on the back to see what it is in the process of giving up. This, no more and no less: It is giving up its academic authority, and giving it to those it is supposed to be in the process of teaching, and (as at San Francisco State College) to a noisy segment of the community, in this case the black militants.

Consider the student sit-ins of the past couple of years. The typical scene took place at the University Placement Service, on the campus. A gang of students decided that the Dow Chemical Company should be impeded in its annual recruitment activity on campus, because it manufactures napalm which is used in the Viet Nam war. They form a mob which prevents normal operation of the interviews, and perhaps they forcibly prevent the Dow interviewer from leaving the room for a few hours. A Dean is imprisoned with the Dow man.

A normal citizen thus kidnapped or imprisoned telephones the police if he can, but this was not the initial reaction of the Dean in question. Bring police on campus? Terrible thought; the campus must be preserved from such intercourse with the dirty world outside. Punish the students later? Certainly not. The President, and the Dean, might *like* to but the faculty won't have it. The students were acting in good conscience and from high idealism. It is true that kidnapping is wrong; but isn't genocide in Viet Nam worse? Besides, if one were to expel the students some of them would lose their deferments and get drafted. I have heard one professor in a faculty meeting say he would not vote a resolution threatening expulsion for second offenders of this sort because that would be to threaten a death sentence in Viet Nam.

The most typical faculty reaction, in the early days of these demonstrations, was to suggest the placement office be moved off campus; there the problem would evaporate. It was discovered, by these faculty members, that placement interviews were not really part of the academic process, and so had no business on the hallowed campus grounds anyway. Of course, such recruitment had been going on for thirty years without noticeable erosion of those professors' scholarly objectivity, freedom, dignity and wealth. But in 1967, under a sudden pressure from a very local public--the militant anti-war students--the evil was discovered exactly where inconvenience lay. And yet these objective scholars continued to type out letters of recommendation for their own students, right on campus, on Department stationery, with no sense of inconsistency.

In 1967 the faculty of Columbia College decided formally that the Registrar's office was no longer to compile a certain statistic known as 'class rank'. For many years every student would find on his academic transcript a statement to the effect that he stood 88th (say) in his class of 972 students. When he applied for a job, or for graduate school, and requested this record be sent to impress the recipient, the class rank went along with his grades and letters of recommendation. Why, precisely in 1967, was this information deemed unworthy of notice? Because, under the draft law of that time it was one measure by which Selective Service distinguished persons whose deferment was 'in the public interest'.

It was a student-initiated objection to military service and the draft, and to the Viet Nam War, which suddenly caused a good many professors to scurry round for sound academic reasons why class rankings were false and misleading. Ranking has no place in the student-faculty pursuit of truth, they argued, only some of them coming right out with the truth that this was being done to sabotage the draft law.

I am not here arguing that the draft law, then or now, was a good one, or even that sabotaging it was a bad thing to do. Nor do I defend or attack the Viet Nam war. I only wish to point out how readily faculties can deceive themselves into believing they are exercising dispassionate judgments about campus affairs from an academic point of view, defending their freedom to teach and learn against all enemies, when in fact they are doing no such thing. A year later, when the new draft law no longer involved class rank in its calculations, all those faculties which had, around the country, been slower than Columbia's in realizing the academic undesirability of class rankings, found the demand for change in *their* Registrar's procedures had vanished. They then had no difficulty forgetting the whole invidious injustice; they had the relationship between their College and the Defense Department to consider instead. Forgetting that in 1944 everyone was proud of the military research on the campuses, they are now discovering that truth cannot survive where physics is partly financed by the AEC.

Had it been up to the faculties, several buildings of Columbia University would be occupied and barricaded to this very day. In the spring of 1968 the professors met in the round-the-clock sessions to find some compromise between good and evil which would placate the evil, but of course they found nothing. Had not the President finally called the police, there would be no Columbia. And it is no different in Cuba, Albania or the Congo, despite the lessons of Mao. Yet to hear some faculties, you would think it was police which destroyed the peace on Morningside Heights. President Kirk had to resign, of course, after unleashing such police brutality; he could no longer command the respect of his courageous faculty, a faculty willing to revile the police, the mayor, and LBJ, but unwilling to call a campus hoodlum anything but his cherished student.

To faculties of this persuasion, police constitute the 'outside interference in campus affairs', while a gang of students pursuing a national plan of disruption is not interference at all.

But that was mild. The Columbia Students were still only attacking the periphery. A Registrar procedure, a new gymnasium--these are still not central. That was last year.

San Francisco State is now suffering a much greater threat to the idea that the faculty is the University, that academic decisions are made by academic men. Indeed, it is not just a threat; the battle is already lost. The 'Black Community' has decided that its eighteen-year olds should go to college, whatever they may or may not have learned up to that age, in as great numbers as they wish, with substantial scholarship aid. It has further decided that since entrance requirements as the academics have heretofore conceived them are irrelevant, so should be the graduation requirements. Let black men work at black studies, taught by black men chosen by black children. Let the degrees, of course, be still called BA, MA and Ph.D. This proposition has largely been accepted by what passes for the Academy in San Francisco.

The BA given for all this should not be subject to the scrutiny of the rest of the College; this too is one of the Demands. One wonders why the old-fashioned degree is even wanted. What can it be worth, under the circumstances? The truth is that Black Studies can be carried on anywhere. A strong voice in the white activist camp argues, indeed, that such things as sociology and politics should be studied in an 'action setting', on the streets of the city. Never mind the old degrees.

The whites can afford to say this; their parents all have degrees, and they aren't worried about jobs. The Blacks know better. It is clear today that certain jobs can't be had without high school diplomas, which today often represent very little even in the way of technical literacy. To the depressed ghetto resident success in life comes from status, or so it appears, not the other way round. Even the *teachers* in ghetto schools are often sadistic illiterates or time-servers. Why deprive Black kids of the certificate to success? If, at the same time, the children have a prideful curriculum in black history and culture, which nobody wants put down, what better combination can there be? Add scholarships and stipends and the package has universal appeal. It seems so reasonable to the ministers, editors and politicians of the black community, who do not wish to be behind Black Panthers for love of their brothers anyhow, that any *academic* objection to the idea is dismissed out of hand as racism or guild self-interest.

One of the pitiful things about the Convocation at San Francisco State, before it collapsed, was the urgency with which the faculty and President Smith were trying to convince the militants that they were doing all they could to open enrollments to the unprepared, so long as they were black, and to expand the Black Studies program. They were, too, but to no avail. The militants were led by people to whom Black Studies, or any studies, meant no more than class rankings meant to the SDS. Thus the battle is joined on a truly anarchist level, faculties trying hard to concede what the opposition doesn't really care about, except as a handle for strife.

And the faculty is puzzled that a 'compromise' is so hard to reach. But who among them has raised the question about whether these proposed 'gains' for the black community really represent gains in education, or productivity? And who among them has raised, apart from the issue on the table, the question of academic freedom, asking that his academy not be stampeded by an ignorant public (won't they admit any more that the public is more ignorant than themselves?) into accepting and certifying as scholarship this particular novelty, forced down their throats with bricks, fire and bombs?

It may be that Black Studies is worth a Department, even if not in every college. There are Institutes of Oceanography, valuable indeed, even if most colleges don't have them. In fact, everything which *is,* is worth study somewhere, by someone. But the question of priorities has to be settled first, and this question has two aspects.

First, the academic or intellectual value of the new program must be considered by academics, and rated. Second, those who have the money to implement such a program must be convinced that it is money better spent in this way than in some other way. There is no escaping these two linked considerations, whether we live in a democracy or a tyrrany, with a capitalist or socialist economy, and whether the College is State or privately financed. What *is* the program, and what is it worth, compared to alternate uses for the same money.

In a State College, politics must necessarily enter the debate, in that 'politics' means the will of the people who pay. Many a professor mindlessly denies this proposition, when he says the politicians should leave the College alone. They can't; even 'leaving it alone' is one method of deciding it should be run in a certain way rather than some other. At the very least, the politician has to decide how much of the people's money should be spent there. He can't do this without hearing a clear and independent academic voice, and that voice, in turn, must be informed by an understanding of what is financially possible.

But the academic who fondly imagines he is forming non-political judgments is at the same time knuckling under to the 'people's voice' with pride and passion. Not the voice heard through the Legislature of Governor; no, he doesn't seem to believe in that sort of democracy. He hears the nearer voice of the BSU, backed by elements outside the College whose understanding of the academy is as weak as its enthusiasm for the democratic process.

One of the black slogans, which puncutated many of the rally speeches, is 'Power to the people!' It would be given at the end of a paragraph, when the speaker ran dry for a moment, in much the same tone, partly perfunctory and partly religious, as the 'Heil Hitler' of 1944, or the 'Hallelujah' of the camp meeting.

But power to what people? The frictions are well known, in our imperfect democracy, by which we often do not get legislatures which do the majority bidding, but these provide no sanction for the 'participatory democracy' which the activists on campus seek to impose. Perhaps our populace is deceived as to the nature of justice, perhaps it is bamboozled by the papers and TV, perhaps it misjudges the candidates for office, but at least it is the whole populace. Oh but they feel democratic at the SDS or BSU meeting when they take a vote on which campus building to sack next, but *I* didn't ask them to vote; that's not democracy for anybody but them. They have no right to vote for me, even if they think, even if they are right in thinking, that they are enlightened and moral, while I am an apathetic imbecile.

It is partly the high moral tone of these participatory types which has paralyzed the academics into paying them more attention than they are worth. There is also, of course, American sentimentality about Youth, and the guilt of the white and affluent at the sight of the ghetto, and finally, I suspect, a deep-down uncertainty the academic often feels about the value of his own work. So that's what President Smith and his faculty, who were fairly well united, did: They listened to the voice of the faction as if it were the voice of the people, and they feared the power of the hoodlums as if it were the power of the people.

And when I say they feared the *power* of these people, I mean precisely their physical, coercive, rock-throwing, gun-wielding power. Such a fear is so new in the American academy that it is hardly surprising that the first reaction is to disarm, to turn the other cheek, and of course to find sound academic reasons to do these things. After a few turnings, at San Francisco State (as at Columbia), there were no cheeks left to turn. The Convocation, during which they gave away about all the academic authority they owned, ended with their being insulted and spurned. President Smith was at that moment trying to get the Trustees to provide him with a few more cheeks to offer, but they refused, and he resigned. Undemocratic Trustees vs. democratic BSU? We are forgetting the basis of our liberties.

Unnoticed at his inauguration was Acting President Hayakawa's announcement that *he* believed the militants were asking too *little*. By this he meant that the black community had, in fact, a right to more and better services from San Francisco State College than a mere Black Studies Department. That much is true, and worth saying, but since he didn't say he was granting the sillier Demands among the fifteen, it all sounded like hogwash in the newspapers, and it was soon buried in the police actions of the following weeks.

Now it is January 1, 1969. Nobody knows what will happen next week. It is possible that a building will be blown up; it is possible that people will be killed. Maybe a combination of teachers' strike and violence will close the place down indefinitely, like the Sorbonne. Maybe the Mayor, or the mediators, will pull off some sort of miracle. Or maybe the firm stand of Hayakawa--no, probably no miracles at all. But whatever happens, however it all turns out, the academic profession will from now on have a hard time convincing itself again that it is free, autonomous, actuated by academic considerations only, resistent of the vile pressures of an unenlightened world. It will have a hard time, but it will succeed.

Learning Twice

ONE OFTEN hears things like "You learn something new every day." Ecclesiastes, on the other hand, has it that "*there* is no new *thing* under the sun." Which is right? Maybe both, when considered properly.

I received in the mail recently a little pamphlet published by the Mathematical Association of America, which explained how to teach mathematics. Hints on, anyway. To avoid insult, no doubt, the introduction said the book was "mainly for younger teachers," but I read it anyway. Younger than who? I thought. Ecclesiastes? Maybe there would be something new to me at least. And sure enough, after a long recital of unexceptionable and familiar sentiments I found a section headed by the following epigraph:

"To teach is to learn twice."
-----Joseph Joubert, *Pensées.*

Quel beau sentiment! Whatever sort of *penseur* Joubert may have been---his name was new to me---he must have been a teacher too, for every teacher knows this, that we have never learned anything so well as when we have had to teach it. In fact, it has often seemed to me that I never really understood anything until I had taught it to someone else.

But if this were true, then what Joubert would have had me---through teaching---learning twice, I was in fact only really learning for the first time, i.e. once. Hm. Paradox like this can only lead to trouble, and so I turned my thoughts in a new direction.

Joseph Joubert, whatever he was, surely wrote that sentence in praise of teaching (What author of a book of *pensées* would knock teaching?): therefore he must have considered it a good thing to learn twice. Indeed, he must have considered it so obviously a good thing, such a pleasure, such a blessing, so primary a reward of teaching, that it didn't occur to him to explain it. He could have written, "To teach is to learn twice, and that's twice as much fun as learning once," which is of course what he meant, but the added clause would have struck him as superfluous.

Me, too; but not everyone. I have met people who don't even want to learn once, much less do they glory in a second go-round. Such people could be in the majority; our democracy may well be ruled by them. Any democracy.

This doesn't bear thinking of, and the slender evidence of the epigraph indicates that Joubert too didn't waste time on so disturbing a possibility. What fine students Joubert must have had, what spirited friends, that the pleasure of "learning twice" was to him so self-evidently understandable. Was he married, I wondered?

****

Wife: You turn left on Berkeley Street.
Husband: I know, I know!
Wife: Well I only wanted to make sure you didn't pass it.
Husband: Don't you give me credit for anything?
Wife: *Any*thing? Look, you passed it last time.

So it goes, This particular husband clearly didn't want to learn twice, at least not behind the wheel. Now put his wife behind the wheel, with himself in the other seat, and see how delicious it becomes (to him) to learn twice---by teaching.

Husband: You turn left at Berkeley Street.
Wife: Yes, dear.
Husband: 'Cause last time you went all the way to Alexander.
Wife: Sorry, dear.
Husband: Well then, O.K. Or---no---it wasn't the last time. Last time you turned on Goodman, remember?
Wife: Yes, dear.
Husband: Or was it Oxford? Goodman or Oxford, anyhow.

Chalk one up for the pleasures of teaching. A true-born teacher never tires of his subject.

****

To every *thing there* is a season, and a time to every purpose under the heaven. Sometimes I find it necessary to tell a class something some of them don't know, though most of them have studied it before: some piece of mathematical information so important to the subject at hand that I can't go on without being sure first that everybody has it straight. Yet I do not wish to insult or bore the majority who (not being teachers themselves, like me and Joubert) might have some objection to learning twice. In such cases I often introduce my lecture like this:

"Many of you already know what I am about to tell you, but some of you do not. Those who do know, please be patient. I am going to explain The Law of Cosines, which you may very well have learned in school somewhere, but if so there is still no need for you to be either bored or insulted.

"Try, rather, to look on what I say as if I were giving a performance, as if this classroom were a theater or concert-hall. My subject is beautiful even if it is familiar; I hope I shall deliver it in a style that doesn't destroy the beauty. If I give a bad performance you have a right to complain, but to complain merely of having heard The Law of Cosines before is like complaining of having heard the Beethoven Quartet Opus 131 before.

"Maybe the simile is extreme, but The Law of Cosines is in fact a lovely monument to the human intellect, and a competent performance of a thing of beauty should always be a pleasure to its audience. Indeed, those of you who already know it should enjoy it more than will those of your classmates who, not having your experience behind them, will have to strain their powers to follow me this first time around."

And then I go on with it. I do try to make the performance one of concert quality, but not entirely for the reason advertised in my little talk.

I know from experience, you see, that precious few of those students actually do understand The Law of Cosines. Many think they do, having heard the words before, or even having made a calculation by it in high school somewhere; these might therefore tune out on what would be a valuable lesson, did I not give them a second self-respecting reason for listening.

A teacher must sometimes be devious. Sure, one can always clobber them with exams, but as the Preacher saith, wisdom *is* better than weapons of war.

Chapter III: **Tales and Fantasies**

The Bulgarian Economist

IT IS probably best not to mention the name of the actual conference we were attending, or the Eastern European country it was held in, except that it was not Bulgaria. Therefore I shall speak of the protagonist--who was not Bulgarian, but who was an official of our host country--as a Bulgarian. All other persons and events are true *mutatis mutandis.* The year was some time in the decade 1970-1979.

Our host, the Bulgarian economist, spoke a fluent English. A respected public official at home, he was equally well-known abroad. He had been Chairman of an International Congress some years before, and was a member of innumerable cross-cultural commissions, the sort of thing that gets financed by UNESCO or the Carnegie Endowment, meets in Nice or the Mazurian Lakes during the appropriate season, and issues Reports. These get circulated widely among embassies and research libraries, but are seldom commented on in the Cincinnati Enquirer.

His mathematical work was said to command the respect of his profession. In earlier years he had made some curiously original applications of the mathematical theories of 'queuing' and 'random walk' to problems of economics as these problems are understood in socialist countries. Most of this work antedated his rise in the bureaucracy. What he had done more recently, apart from attending International Congresses, was not known to us.

Not that we ourselves were exactly mathematical economists. There were five of us at the table: our Bulgarian host, a Hungarian mathematician, a Japanese government official (educated at the University of Chicago Business School), a Canadian computer scientist and myself. Economic problems were our common meeting ground, and none of us was a stranger to the language and method of econometrics, but the point of the Conference we were attending was precisely that the participants be somehow peripheral to that science and yet able (presumably) to contribute to it.

We all spoke English, at the Conference and at the table that night. Our host regaled us with the Eastern European analogue of "risqué" stories, i.e. quips at the expense of socialist doctrine, or bureaucratic practise, in Russia. About his own country he would only smile a bit, but the heavier pages of Marx and Hegel (Germans, after all) could also safely come in for a bit of goodnatured ribbing.

As the wine went round again he turned more serious. "I am thinking to write a book," he said, "Or maybe someone younger than I should do it---it does not matter who, but it is something that should be done. I would wish to start it, at least."

"The idea is mathematical at bottom, but it could turn out to be a profound model for the reality we see about us everyday. A symmetry principle of a sort. Consider:

"You know how you in the West describe your two sorts of inflation? 'Cost-push' is one kind, and--how do you say it? 'Demand-pull'? Something like that. I believe it was this very terminology that gave me the idea I speak of, probably because of the way it comes out in Bulgarian," and here he said something in Bulgarian that did indeed have a sort of duple meter and musical quality.

"You see, it has a poetic virtue, this opposition of your two problems, as if the solution might be found by somehow averaging the extremes. Or, as in Hegel, by means of a synthesis where previously all was in conflict. However, inflation is not the subject of my book.

"What I wish to do is to analyze the operation of a certain sort of economy: an economy in which there is a chronic excess of demand."

He spoke those last words slowly and carefully; "chronic excess of demand" was the key, no doubt about it. But what did it mean? An economy whose citizens desired more than they could afford? Who has heard of any other kind of economy? (A Trappist monastary, perhaps.)

"By *chronic,* I mean 'all the time'," our host went on. You in the West don't have this situation. Oh I know, sometimes you have in some shop completely sold out of a certain item, which must then be ordered while the customer waits. Or your recurrent 'credit crunch', which is to say a shortage of mortgage money for builders and so on. But these are not the rule in the West. Ordinarily you are in a condition I would call 'chronic oversupply' of goods and services.

"Look at your department stores. Their shelves are almost always filled with unsold goods, waiting for customers to come in with some money in their pockets. Look at your automobile showrooms and parking lots, vast numbers of cars not being used, waiting. When someone arrives saying he might buy one, think of the relief of the clerk, of the owner of the franchise!

"Now in our country--in the socialist states in general, according to my observation--there is a perfectly opposite but symmetric state that I will call 'excess of demand.' Again, we too have our exceptions, I'll grant you that, just as your 'chronic excess of supply' has its exceptions. For example, I have seen a shipment of tennis shoes come in to our main downtown department store, or a truckload of amber bead necklaces, which then do not get sold for ever so long a time. Yes, they stand on the shelf like your Fords and Chevrolets, wasting time, wasting 'interest charges on inventory' if you'll permit me a capitalist description.

But *in general,* while your goods wait on the shelves for the consumers, here the consumers speak first. They sign up on a subscription list--for an apartment, a washing-machine--before the supply appears, not afterwards. For smaller things--food, clothing--there is never too much on our shelves. Whatever the people need that day--no more. Indeed, the customer often reaches the counter and finds there not quite what he wanted; he explains to the clerk, the clerk to the supervisor, and so on up the line until the proper productive machinery is placed into operation. It is thus the voice of the people that determines the proportions of production, not (as with you) the reverse.

"There is perhaps another way to model the phenomenon I speak of. As in any microeconomic linear programming problem, the optimum looked for is subject to several constraints, at least according to the model. When the solution is found, however, it is often discovered that most of the apparent constraints were in fact irrelevant: one of the inequalities involved might as well have been an equality.

"This, I propose, is the situation in both our systems. What do we wish to maximize? Gross National Product, prosperity, in a word. Or, in another word, Production. (You will forgive me if I speak purely as an economist and ignore such values as love, peace, religion. For the moment let us talk as if only 'production' matters.)

"The constraints on production, that is, on putting material of value into the hands of consumers who want that material, are many, and any of you can name half a dozen: raw material availability, labor skill, transportation. . . But the ones that operate in the socialist economy all appear on one side: supply. If we *had* more shirts, houses, beefsteaks, and busses going to the Crimea, we would *immediately* have more people using these things. The constraint on our prosperity is excess of demand, or shortage of supply, however you wish to emphasize it.

"With you it is another part of the graph. People will not of course consume more than they demand (I use 'demand' in its technical sense). If you can generate more demand, you will be more prosperous. The maximum point of the GNP function invariably is found along your demand boundary condition, and not along any of the other bounding planes, like supply.

"Both of our economies seek to push back our respective bounding conditions.

"In your case, your productive agencies first make certain guesses as to what the people want, and they hope--or manipulate--that the distribution of money for the purpose will also be to their advantage. Then they seek to persuade the potential buyers. They advertise, they put fins on automobiles, they make a dozen different models of toaster, some with less, some with more, chromium plating. As if this made a difference in anything but the pushing back of the demand-shortage bounding condition on our programming diagram!

"I do not speak of the 'morality' of all this; believe me, gentlemen, I speak only technical matters, and I speak just as frankly of our own Bulgarian situation, where our own chronic shortage is not demand, as we who have studied the matter are able to prove. Yes, gentlemen, we too have our shortages.

"You see therefore the symmetry that relates these two sorts of economy. From a mathematical point of view the analysis should be very much the same, though of course the social consequences are quite different. We would never wish to give up our mode of production, 'production for use, not for profit,' as we say, in favor of the opposite system; but as a matter of study they are almost the same thing. With us, chronic excess demand; with you, chronic excess supply. When the proper equations are written for the analysis of an economy of chronic excess demand, we will only have to interchange x and y to convert it into the corresponding analysis of chronic excess supply.

"Such is the magic of mathematics, my friends, that in diversity one may find an essential unity. How little valuable are the complications of moral judgement when we pursue a neutral truth! The older thinkers--Marx, Lenin--visualized a new world growing inexorably out of the past, in a progress from feudalism through capitalism and socialism to a morally ideal communism whose time has even now not yet arrived. But the language they used was obscure, filled with words, with philosophy as the nineteenth century understood such things. The result has been a confused pursuit, along an uncertain path where, as in the fairy-tales, one monster suddenly appears to be two, where disguise is the only reality. Poetry is not dispensible, that is sure, but it is not the language of our science; it is not the mode--as you say in computer science--in which the machine of economic and historical understanding will operate.

We waste our time in puzzling over the unquantifiable, 'the quality of life', or 'liberty', or 'privilege' or 'equality'. What are these things? As your philosopher Marcuse has shown, even tolerance is a form of repression. Words can be twisted; there is in the twisting to be found no light, "nor certitude, nor peace, nor help from pain." Surely that is not the way to understand what has brought us here.

"A mathematical principle is another matter. 'God said, "Let Newton be," and all was light.' Did Newton ask whether it was better that the sun pull on the earth than that the earth pull on the sun? More just, more free? There are truths that stand apart from such ideas. They are not always so grand as the law of universal gravitation, but all truth is beautiful, and truths mathematically expressed lead us out from the umbrous thicket of words and into the light. I would hope this to be the case with the economic principle of symmetrical 'shortage'.

"As I see it, there is an isomorphism between our two systems, a single system of constraints upon happiness that we all enjoy equally--or suffer from equally--not in the absolute of course, but by a mathematical transformation. If we are constrained by x, so you are constrained by y, neither more nor less. In both cases the optimum is found exactly along the line of constraint. There is no difference--no difference at all except for the name of the constraint. With a stroke of the pen we may put x for y and y for x, and so interchange, as it were, life in Bulgaria for life in Denmark.

"Yes indeed. Bulgaria for Denmark! A simple transformation, an isomorphism. Isn't that so, Janos?" He slapped Janos on the shoulder. "Yes old friend, Hungary too. The mathematics is as good for Hungary as for Bulgaria. What shall be your transformation? x for z perhaps? x for logarithm of z? I'll give you Holland for Hungary! Holland, Janos;

think of it, old friend! Gouda cheeses, as many as you can eat, beer instead of dishwater, German automobiles, kindly policemen, cafés with newspapers from all over Europe every morning with that rich Dutch chocolate and hot fresh milk!

"So easy, Janos! Just put x for y, or maybe logarithm of y. A stroke of the pen--no more!"

Janos stared at the floor, nor did he laugh. The rest of us were stunned. A waiter in balloon pants came up to ask something of our host, who replied briefly in Bulgarian and, as the waiter went off again, rose from the table.

"It is all taken care of, gentlemen; no need to pay. The wine was good, yes?"

Here the economist raised his glass into the air as if in a toast to an absent deity, and, speaking no word, drained it and set it down again.

"My pleasure, gentlemen. You cannot know what a privilege it is to be among you. Now we must sleep if we are to hear Koopman in the morning. Yes, the morning. You will tell me then what you think of my little idea. There will be plenty of time tomorrow, I think. Good night, my friends, good night."

News in Depth

(Consisting of two Interviews, separated by one Public Service Announcement, as broadcast on National Civic Radio, a non-profit network of the people.)

AND NEXT we will have a report on the results of the International Monetary Conference in Brussels. Leda Wermer will tell us about the Conference. What *were* the results of the International Monetary Conference in Brussels, Belgium, Leda?

"Well, Simon, as you know, there was held last week an International Monetary Conference in Belgium, at which representatives of both the industrial and underdeveloped nations were present. It was truly an international conference, gathered in Brussels, at which all points of view were fully aired.

"As might be expected, the speeches centered on the monetary problems in the world's economy. Of course, many of the problems were quite technical, Simon, dealing with such little-understood matters as exchange rates and balance of payments, but if one were to summarize the *essence* of what was said, one would have to divide the presentations into two parts:

"On the one hand, there are all the underdeveloped nations whose principal concern is development, and who are anxious to create an international monetary order which will promote development, especially in the underdeveloped countries. This group, Simon, tends to view the industrialized nations (especially the US and Western Europe, but also, to some extent, the Soviet Union and the Eastern European socialist states) with a certain amount of distrust. They are looking for a structure of payments that will promote their own development, but they fear that any such structure will be vetoed by what they regard as the representatives of the self-interested, especially multi-national corporations of the West. They feel that if they could somehow break through this barrier of mistrust, misunderstanding, self-interest and exploitation, some of it going back hundreds of years, there might be some basis for the negotiation of a more just and stable international monetary community.

"The representatives of the industrial powers, on the other hand, tended to be more restrained (ha, ha) in their enthusiasm for reform. The third secretary of the American delegation, for example, Mr. Burton Fuller, who has had a long and distinguished career in The Mobil Oil Company, said nothing at all on this question. The American spokesman, in a prepared statement, urged caution on the delegates. I would say his speech was intentionally a little vague, but in brief he seemed to be saying that Rome wasn't built in a day."

Tell me, Leda, *does* it look as though the Western powers are going to submit to any reform that would make a meaningful change in the way international currency speculations affect the deprived and the underdeveloped?

"Fundamentally, Simon, the answer is probably no. Of course, Western economists argue that the reforms proposed by certain Third World emerging nations are unrealistic, and don't measure up to what they call the hard facts of life--and they may have a point there--but fundamentally the answer to your question is no."

Is there any hope at all, then?

"Well, Simon, there is always hope. The International Conference on Monetary Reform is going to meet again in 6 months' time, this time in Luanda. It may be that the seriousness of the problem will have been brought home to the conferees in such a way that a new try can be made. And of course the elections in America will be over, with perhaps a more sympathetic Administration."

Well, thank you Leda. That was a very informative report. We look forward to hearing from you again.

"Thank you Simon. Good night."

Good night, Leda. After a brief pause for station identification, National Civic Radio, an unsponsored, listener-supported network, will bring you an in-depth report on what promises to be an exciting development in the world of art: The Webster Festival.

****

The following message is presented as a public service of Station CPTA in cooperation with your State and County Departments of Consumer Affairs, part of a continuing series of consumer bulletins created by the CPTA Consumer Task Force to provide the individual citizen with the information he or she needs to cope with an increasingly complex environment.

Intelligent comparison shopping can help reduce the high cost of food. Look for the *specials* advertised in your local newspapers; very often you can save up to ten percent or more on your weekly grocery bill by making a careful selection of certain items discounted to attract customers. Be sure to buy your meats and vegetables in stores with the lowest prices, for otherwise you will be spending your grocery money unnecessarily.

Fruits and vegetables in season usually offer the best buys, and if you find beef or fish too expensive, it may pay you to try pork or poultry instead. By not buying the expensive cuts you will, in addition, be helping to bring down their prices. This is a public service announcement. Art Time next.

****

Good evening, this is Art Time on National Civic Radio, and we have with us in the studio Mr. Werther Wermer of the New York State Citizen's Commissioin on the Arts. Welcome, Werther, glad to see you again.

"Glad to be here Simon."

Well, Werther, it seems as if we've been hearing of little else but the Webster Festival these past few days. Is it open yet?

"Oh yes, indeed, Simon. In fact, it has been open for months, in a sense, Simon. But seriously, it opened to the public last Thursday, August 7th."

Open for months? How do you mean?

"Well, Simon, some of the displays aren't quite what one might expect, ha, ha, but I'll get on to that in a minute. First let me describe what some of the preparations were and what you can expect to see when you come down to Artfair Forum.

"Take first Rick Waackle's *Main Street Realty in Time & Space,* a series of photographs of all the buildings in downtown San Gimigniano, New Jersey. These are mounted on the north walls of Galleries 1, 2 and 3, there are ninety-seven in all. This work reaches beyond its physical presence in the gallery to derive its significance from its interaction with society--gathering its frenzy from the public and feeding it back symbiotically, as predicted by Darwin and confirmed by Fichte and R.

D. Laing."

Let me interrupt for just a moment, Werther. Rather than get any deeper into Waackle's work just now, perhaps you could give us a rundown on what the Webster Festival at Artfair Forum this year is all about. Just a birdseye view, so to speak.

"Well certainly, Simon. Summer at Artfair Forum is full of surprises. It's a blend of art and leisure that's never been tried before, a place for new ideas and outdoor fun, a way to bring arts closer to the way we live.

"Art is for the *people,* Simon; I do hope we've got over that old idea that you have to be specially *educated,* or pull a long *face,* to appreciate it. Art is *nature,* after all, and it isn't just visual. Children will love the storytellers and troubadours, who are there almost every day, and there are demonstrations of jousting and bread-making almost constantly.

"Much of what we do is in the healthy outdoors, where the visitor can walk and look at the artists actually at work. Ju Whimpl, for example, composes her sculptures on the face of the Artfair cliffs, using the natural movements of wind and water to shape the result. And what is most exciting, you see, is that there *is* no final result! Ju's sculpture is always in *process,* never in *progress.* Therefore it doesn't matter at all when you come to see it.

"Then of course Artist Jonathan Suger will grow his grass sculpture from the Greek Theater to the Eastern Gate. Designer Solomonescue will be seen conferring with a group of poets and engravers on an Artfair Webster Festival Memorial Volume, and Rosalie Tomkin will form her human jigsaw puzzles from whatever material comes her way."

Aleatoric sculpture?

"Exactly, Simon! And there will be film making, printmaking and winemaking lessons for all guests. All in all, Simon, a very *exciting* place to be."

But tell me, Werther, what was that absolutely *tantalizing* hint you let drop a minute ago when you said that this year's Webster Festival had actually in some sense been open for months?

"Oh *that,* well, there is a sense, Simon, in which the Webster Festival at Artfair Forum has been open longer than it has been open. And if that sounds like a paradox, it is.

"To take just one example: On February 29, 1976, Larry Roberts carried a single ice cube from his apartment on Haight and Scott Streets in San Francisco to the Golden Gate Park, where he lost it. Since that time it has certainly melted, and in part evaporated.

"Now Artfair Forum is less than three thousand miles from the Golden Gate Park, and there were billions and billions of water molecules in Larry's ice cube. Larry has calculated, with his collaborator Jurgen Himmelfarb, who teaches mathematics at the Mount Olympus Community college, that at least 7000, and perhaps as many as 600,000 molecules are within the very precincts of Artfair Forum, this very day!

"Thus Larry Roberts' art is real but invisible you see. He influences space and atmosphere through the discharge of energies. His work has filled Artfair Forum with an emanation no less formful for having been unformed, and no less formless for having been, er, released, as it were, and expanding spherically through the entire universe.

"Yet the visitor should know it is *there,* and that it is one among the many influences which, with the generous assistance of the New York Council on the Arts, we hope will transform our daily lives just a little in the direction of nature, health and love."

Well, that *is* exciting, Werther. Thank you very much. And be sure to come back again soon, now, hear?

"Thank *you,* Simon, it was great being here. I do hope I've been of some service in pointing out to the general public what their public servants are doing for them in the realm of art. That's what we're here for, after all."

And a good thing you *are*, Werther. But you must be very busy, so I won't keep you any longer. This is Simon Wilson, your host for *One Person's Meat,* a daily feature of National Civic Radio. I will return in a moment with an editorial opinion. (Music up and out.)

Prize-Day Ceremony at the Hydro-Electric Institute

The Chairman speaks.

THE TASK of your Committee has been made particularly difficult this year by the fact of the large field of egregiously well-qualified young scientists we had to choose from. The originality and technological relevance of the work presented for our judgement is unparallelled in my eleven years' experience in this task. It augurs well for the future of hydro-electric engineering in this country, and indeed everywhere, that we should have had the privilege of judging among fifteen such brilliant examples, such dedicated examples, of the erg-monger's art.

Fortunately there were three prizes available. Before announcing the winner of the grand prize, I shall name all three and describe their work briefly. In alphabetical order, the winners are Jack Baker, Michele Livorno, and Homer Twang.

Jack Baker is the author of a round dozen papers in the metadynamics of continuous-flow pseudo-oscillators. He is now preparing a major review of the literature in this often reviled (because misunderstood) technology, and it will soon be published by the Totenwissenschaft Verlag of Toledo, Ohio.

Baker's most recent paper, "The Nominal Three" (with an epigraph from Duns Scotus), contemplates an elastic medium the nature of which is to extend beyond its object source into space. His experiment (a *gedanken* experiment, needless to say) denies the limitations of traditional fluid mechanics, and by the negation of a bounding framework casts loose the prejudices of form.

Michele Livorno, on the other hand, has occupied herself with analysis in the small. Her major work, "Discrepancy factors energize the total," makes intimate use of hitherto unrecognized moving frames, physically separated, blunt and inert, in combinations and *re*combinations that force upon our consciousness those famous words of Thomas Babbage that are needless to repeat before this audience.

But, unlike Babbage, Michele Livorno has assembled a *public* theory, minimal to be sure, but drawing its meaning from its very interaction with the practising hydro-electric engineer. Thus, too, are her terrific calorific conceptualizations carried forward, not in themselves, but in their otherness, the practical benefits of which will surely accrue to generations quite unborn.

Our third prizewinner, Homer Twang, has for full five years been creating an aleatoric *schema* for the penultimate analysis of astatic hydro-chemical reactivators. Twang's theory is not aleatoric in the sense that it applies synthetic probability considerations to an objective reality; that much is traditional.

Instead, the uncertainty inheres in his theoretical structure itself. *Is* it a theory? *Is* it a structure? "Structure" may not, indeed, be the proper rubric for a scientific experience so immanent in its communicated concretion. Twang's proposals *must* be communicated, for their reality apart from their hazardous transmission is dubious.

Scientific theories and experiments so intellectually incomprehensible possibly present difficulties to other engineers. They might even seem private to the researcher. To think this would, however, be a great mistake on the part of any forward-looking hydro-electric utility. It must be understood that the breakdown of the limits of engineering *forms* as a consequence opens up the engineering *experience.*

Nowhere is this more true than in hydro-electric engineering. It is to the credit of the industry that its leaders have recognized this truth, and have persuaded the consumers of hydro-electric power (via the various State Public Service Commissions) to support these researches with generosity and good-will.

The more dematerialized and generalized an experiment becomes, after all, the more encompassing and universal it thereby becomes. Meticulously and simply composed, the work of all three of these fine young engineers attains a personal and collective synthesis of Tschybyschevian precision, but also of Planckian sensibility.

Your Committee has, after careful consideration, decided to present the First Prize to Homer Twang. We cite in particular his paper

"On Canniballs" for its luminosity, weight, and duration. Uniquely among the works presented to this Committee, it engaged our fervor and ferocity. Once the formal parameters of the nonparametric statistics invoked by Twang were seen in all their dim perspective, woven (as it were), or perhaps sprayed, into a sociochemical fabric of uncertain reactions in an unbounded flux, there could be no doubt of the outcome.

[*At this point the Chairman presented the prizes and brought the ceremony to a close.*]

Mexico City, D.F.
January 1, 1974

The government of President Salvador Quinada announced today that it has reached full agreement with the Arab Union and Confederate States delegates to the Fourth World Co-prosperity Conference today, regarding the allocation of oil resources. Details of the system have not yet been published, but informed sources say the quota for the U.S.A. has been abolished altogether, while Western Europe will receive no more than 50% of its 1970-1972 average. Prices too will rise, high enough to offset the reduced volume of production.

The Mexican authorities will seal off at least 25% of all operating wells in the northern province of Texas, indefinitely, as a military reserve. The danger of Yankee military intervention is taken quite seriously despite recent denials from the White House in Baltimore.

Also, in a historic first, it is rumored that a formal non-aggression pact will soon be signed by the Mexican and Confederate States authorities, putting to a formal end the undeclared war of 1932-1939 which established the present demarcation line between the oil-rich Mexican province of Texas, and the Louisiana regions of the CSA. These boundaries were stablized by League of Nations action in 1939 but, though demilitarized since 1940, they have never before been ratified by the Confederacy.

(Venezuela and Canada have not yet joined the oil-producers' alliance, and it is questionable if either will do so. They remain the USA's only two substantial oil sources now that Iran has contracted all its output to the Soviet Union. The Council of Economic Advisors has informed the President that the maximum available imports from these two sources will not suffice to maintain the U.S.A.'s position as 18th in the world in percapita income.)

****

Commentary

by Vernon Woodstock, Professor of History
Forward University

Recent developments in the pattern of world trade have given rise to a number of speculations in the historical profession concerning past U.S. policy in international affairs. At a recent meeting of the American Historical Society there took place an extraordinary symposium entitled *Revising the Past,* in which five papers were presented outlining the probable present situation if each of five historic 19th Century U.S.A. foreign policy decisions had gone the other way. These decisions were:

1) The decision to buy the Louisiana Territory (1803).
2) The decision to permit the Mexican reoccupation of its northwest territories (1849).
3) The decision not to contest secession of The Confederacy (1861).
4) The decision not to buy Alaska (1867).
5) The decision to acquire Cuba, Puerto Rico and the Philippines from Spain (1899).

A school of revisionist historians, calling themselves The Hard-Boiled Eggs, now say most of these decisions, if not all of them, were wrong. The early anti-imperialist philosophy by which we left Alaska to the Russians and avoided war with Mexico and The Confederacy is now seen by this group to have deprived us of access to what could have been a sufficiency of oil, gas and other important natural resources, while it permitted authoritarian governments to oppress those populations whose right to 'self-determination' was the moral basis for our inaction.

Whereas the ideals of the American Revolution of 1776 could have been carried from Maine to California and the Dakotas to the Gulf Coast and Rio Grande, it is said that that we now find more real self-determination in the 'colony' of Manila than in the 'independent republic' of Mexico. On the one hand, the U.S.A. is reviled as 'imperialist' for its acquisition of the Spanish territories which in fact are a great drain on the American economy, and on the other hand we have given away those territories which could have made us prosperous and self-sufficient. Finally, in a wholly unnecessary display of morality, say the Hard-Boiled Eggs, we saved Europe from German imperialism in the 20th Century only to lose it to Russian and Arab blackmail.

Had the United States kept Texas and California, said Professor Eugene V. Mafioso of the University of Western New York, in his paper on the Mexican crisis, we would not now have the degrading spectacle of poverty-striken inhabitants of Utah and Nevada migrating to the rich fruit and vegetable harvests of California, often illegally crossing the border to work at wages below the Mexican legal minimum. Texas cattle could have fed all New England instead of being sent, as they are now, to the wealthier nations of Asia and South America.

Professor Mafioso's paper barely touched on the petroleum question, coming as it did before the formation of the Fourth World alliance, but it did use the statistical-historical techniques recently developed in the revisionist camp to analyze the entire complex of Western Hemisphere trade. The analysis claims that a political and economic union of the USA, Canada, Alaska, the Confederacy and the northern provinces of Mexico, excluding Mexico below the Rio Grande, would have produced a population 50% wealthier on average than today. The average Western New Yorker would have been at double that and at nobody else's expense.

Professor Mafioso's paper was hotly contested by a panel consisting of the humanist Mumble Brown, the historian Laura Banitz and the philosopher Herbert Mancuso. All three criticized the materialist stance of The Hard-Boiled Eggs, and accused them of injuring the *detente* with Mexico which has been the cornerstone of U.S. policy.

"Such a bellicose revisionism," said Professor Brown, "is characteristic of the New England superego, and is itself sufficient to show that political union with the Tropical Powers would have had great difficulty surviving." Professor Brown described the present conflict as having its roots in climate and Puritanism, not in oil or grapes or cattle.

"The superficial (liberal Protestant) view, with its implicit philosophy of progress, identifies Protestantism with the modern age as it identifies Protestantism with capitalism," he explained, "whereas the transcendance of personal neurosis is the dominant task of the age."

Professor Mancuso derided the notion that the U.S.A.---even had it tried---could have made any fundamentally different decision respecting Mexico. "Late industrial society," he said, "has increased rather than reduced the need for parasitical and alienated functions (for the society as a whole, if not for the individual), but wealth inheres in the usevalue of the unadministered life." The social order towards which President Quinada is now moving is, he explained, a post-liberal, phenomenon prefigured by an inevitable 19th Century preparation in which the bourgeois U.S.A. could have had no part.

Professor Banitz, while crediting Mancuso's Bayesian allegory with a suggestive force of no mean dimension, argued that a plain calculation of balance of forces, and not any generosity concerning Texan or Californian self-determination, dictated the retreat of the U.S.A. in 1840, and that that calculation was moreover correct. Washington would certainly have lost any war in the vast deserts of the west, where guerrilla bandits can live untroubled even today. We are fortunate, in fact, that that particular thorn is in Quinada's side, not our own.

Finally, said Professor Banitz, the conquest of Texas would have meant the extension of slavery, with the rise of a class so dependent on slaves that we might never have been persuaded, as we were in 1861, to relinquish the slave-holding part of our Union of that date. Therefore, since slavery was an ineradicable feature of our 1791 Constitution, we might today have found ourselves the last slave-holding nation in the world. Would Professor Mafioso have wanted this?

As moderator of the panel on Professor Mafioso's paper on the Mexican decision, as a participant in the discussion of the 1898 war, and as a spectator of the debates on the other three decisions, I had ample opportunity to hear all sides on these great issues. Any thoughtful historian, I submit, must come to the conclusion that American foreign policy has been more or less correct in these hundred and fifty years. The Louisiana Purchase was justified; France could not in the long run maintain a presence in Louisiana any more than it could in Canada. But a detached Alaska would be silly, and the world would never have tolerated our retaining such a colony, especially once oil was discovered there.

The conflicts with Mexico and the Confederacy would have been as expensive, or worse, than our more recent conflicts with Germany and Japan actually have been. Morality too dictated peace in 1840-1860, just as it dictated war with the later tyrants. New York may not be as wealthy as Mexico City or Atlanta, but we have nothing to reproach ourselves for. With a little more good will on our part we will soon be able to persuade the Tropical Powers that we intend them no harm--doesn't all our history prove it?--and the oil embargo will be lifted.

We have much to offer the world: our musicians and chess-players are supreme, and a Wisconsin girl has just been elected Miss Universe. What is this dream of military glory, of wealth, of great highways in imitation of Texas and Tennessee, of fat steaks and vintage wine? I'll take an Idaho baked potato ahead of any dish the world can offer, and the clean air untainted by gasoline fumes, and the great forests of Michigan and the lobsters of Maine. If this is the Puritan mentality, so be it. We can live at peace with Texans and Russians; what is more important is that this peace permits us to live at peace with ourselves. Salaam Aleikam!

Noblesse Oblige

THE TOWN of Brighton Recycling Center is a group of three corrugated tin sheds on the edge of an unpaved lot marked *Brighton Highway Department.* One shed is for tied bundles of newspaper, one is for tin cans--flattened--and one is for bottles. Separate bins for brown, green and colorless.

The bottle shed has a crazy marquee on stilts; it looks like an army mess-hall in 1944, out where there are rainy seasons. I pulled up at the entrance behind a white Volkswagen whose driver, a lady, had left its engine running. She carried a paper bag--not much of a load. As I followed I saw that she had placed in the 'green' bin two bottles labelled *Chateau Lascombes.*

Lascombes is a fine chateau wine, not the best but certainly good enough. Only a professional would be able to distinguish it from *Chateau Margaux* itself. I had already distributed my own empty bottles before I thought to look for the vintage year on the *Lascombes.* 1970, I thought, but it was hard to tell in the gloom. Other people were entering; it didn't seem right that I should be found scrabbling among the old bottles for a clearer look.

1970 is reputed a year with excellent prospects. I my self haven't yet tried any 1970 Bordeaux, as the year is quite recent for a *grand cru classé.* I have in fact a few *Lascombes* '66 in my own cellar and opened one just last summer. It was still rather rough of course but held promise of real excellence in another few years. Who can be opening a '70?

I turned to look at her more closely, but she had disappeared into her VW. Blowing a last cloud of very blue smoke, she drove out of the recycling center. Her engine needed a tune-up, maybe piston rings. Well, a bit of blue smoke, after all. The important thing is not to clutter up the township with empty Bordeaux bottles. From each according to his ability.

Over the next two days I several times thought of her, "La Dame aux Bouteilles". Other images--almost memories--came to mind. The Vicar's wife in a Victorian village, distributing alms of some sort among the cottagers. Crockery, perhaps, to some grateful family with fewer bowls than mouths to feed.

Did the Vicar's lady leave the engine running? Curious how an image from Trollope should so intertwine one's own experience.

Then I saw her again. Professor, not Vicar; she turned out to be the wife of one of my own colleagues, waiting at the Faculty Club to meet her husband for lunch. She smiled as I entered, as if she knew me, held out a hand--"We meet again"--and introduced herself. I did the same and mentioned something about my (slight) acquaintance with her husband.

"But tell me," I asked, "Those two Chateau Lascombes bottles you had the other morning; were they 1970's?"

"Oh dear," she said, "I can't rightly remember." Her brow furrowed. "I didn't realize we had to separate them by *year.*"

God help me, I was about to reassure her when she gave a merry little laugh and was gone.

Forty Years in the Desert

MY UNCLE Zalman died six years ago; I was not able to go to Detroit for the funeral. My father was there, the last of three brothers who had come to America from Nasielsk between 1913 and 1923. A sister and two other brothers stayed in Poland and did not survive 1944.

Sam, the adventurous one, was the first to leave home. He learned early to speak a fluent English of a sort, which never improved thereafter. Who needed better? He confidently rolled a toothpick around his square mouth, spoke easily of salesmen, washing machines, mortgages--and grew rich. It was Sam who brought his two brothers here--also innumerable nephews and cousins--set them up in business, and regarded himself as patriarch of the new family. He played that role fully, too, even beyond the time of its validity.

My father, for example, also did pretty well in business. When he grew sufficiently prosperous, he began occasioinally to go counter to Sam's advice, and Sam felt injured. Sam preferred his protégés poor. From 1939 or so he and my father didn't get along at all well.

Zalman was the oldest. He was already forty when he reached Detroit, too old, I think, to begin again. Twenty years older, he had been almost a father to my own father's childhood, but in America his wisdom, his experience and his language were as old seeds in a stony soil.

Like his brothers, he opened a store on Chene Street, but it never developed. He spoke Polish to his customers, Yiddish to his family; English stayed forever foreign to him. From his fortieth to his eightieth year he was a lost soul in a strange land.

It was not that he lacked spirit and wit--not at all. One time--it must have been 1928 or so--he was persuaded to take out first citizenship papers. Five years later he found himself for a time studying the English language, and American History, for his citizenship examination. They would ask him about the U.S. Constitution, he was told, and the Emancipation Proclamation. It was a fairy-tale; he made no sense of it. Lincoln was more remote to him than Moses.

Yet, as he later told it, the examination went easily enough.

Whatever the Judge asked him, he had one answer--*Roosevelt.* Who is the Father of Our Country? Roosevelt. Who freed the slaves? Roosevelt. Who is the Governor of Michigan? Roosevelt.

"O.K." said the Judge, "You'll do."

Maybe it didn't happen exactly that way, but Zalman was no fool, and could tell a good story. He did, in fact, vote for Roosevelt and no other, until he gave up voting.

So long, then, as he was a sort of tourist in America, poverty, inability to succeed in business, strangeness of surroundings--all affected him little. Nor did he ever become embittered, even at the end. But his soul stayed in Nasielsk.

Then Nasielsk was destroyed, his roots withered and he knew himself an exile. His wife died, his sons drifted away and his business folded up gently. Sam and my father, quarreling all the while, supplied him with remittances by a formula varying and uncertain. They sustained his business for a time, and ended by sustaining Zalman alone. I think Zalman's second wife also brought him a little money. At any rate, he lived somehow, with always a glass of sweet wine for me when I visited him.

In my childhood Zalman was strong of voice and body. His own man, he was not suffering under Sam's benevolent heel. On Sunday mornings he would come into our house like a whirlwind, scattering snow through the kitchen and shouting for us all to get up and meet the day. He carried a bag of rolls, still warm from Katzen's bakery on Westminster Street, for our breakfast; his own he left in his Model T outside. From his store he might have brought harmonicas for my brother and me, and for my parents he had the current issue of *Der Tag,* the Yiddish newspaper.

"Cold, cold--It's cold outside!" he would shout, and put his hands down my back to show me while I squealed and squirmed away. When things were quieter he would tell us of his lions.

He had two lions, he said, terrific beasts, which he kept tethered on Belle Isle in the Detroit River. Their roar--Zalman would himself roar in illustration--could frighten big boys and policemen, but he didn't often let them roar. He explained to us their size--they towered above the trees--and the great clanking chains by which he kept them in check. How awful it would be if one of the chains broke!

That was 1928. Thirty years later Zalman roared no more. He

lived on Calvert Street in a four-family house, brick, with four little stone porches facing the street, two upstairs and two down. Four rusty mailboxes flanked the dark entrance, whose door, varnished many times over, led to a stairway up the middle of the rigidly symmetrical building. Two apartments at the first landing, two at the top. Uncle Zalman, 79 years old, lived in the lower left.

My father visited him every week; Sam was dead. When I was in Detroit, visiting my parents, I would go along with my father. There was not much I could say in English which Zalman might understand; even my father, in Yiddish, had only platitudes left. How are you, how is your back, it's warm outside, it's cold outside. A duty to an older brother who used to pretend to let him drive the horses in Nasielsk, but who was a quiet old man now from another world.

Two or three times I brought him my own small children, awakening a spark of his former fantasy, but they didn't understand about the lions. They grew restless, Zalman grew tired. His wife gave us wine and cookies, the wine too sweet, the cookies too tough for my children's taste; they dragged me away.

****

We all return in the end, I think, to our earliest values. As tourists in the middle of life we may love our hosts, where we sojourn, and take on, for a time, their manners; but finally, as exiles, we find no comfort there.

In his old age Zalman had become exceedingly religious, like his father before him. True, he had never stopped being observant, he had always kept a Kosher house (unlike my father), but in the last years he became meticulous and intolerant of the laxity of others. He would eat nothing outside his own house. His wife baked his Sunday rolls.

A doctor once prescribed vitamins for him, but before he took any he enquired from Rabbis and Jewish pharmacists whether they were Kosher, and whether flesh and milk in origin. In fact, I do not know for certain that he ever found the answer, or if he took them.

What did he do with his days, Zalman? He said his prayers at sunrise and sunset, as the Law prescribed. He ate his meals, he napped, he read *Der Tag*. He followed avidly the controversies in the Letters column, and sometimes wrote a letter of his own. Twice they were printed. On warm evenings he would sit outside with his neighbors, on folding chairs on the sidewalk, and talk. On Friday nights and Saturday mornings--the Sabbath--he walked to the synagogue, and sometimes on other days as well, as on the anniversaries of family deaths, when special prayers are required.

Two of the other tenants of his house were friends of a sort: Holtz and Berman, Jews, old-timers like himself, perhaps a few years younger. With them he could talk a little, across the porches or out on the sidewalk, of politics and prices. Whatever it was, Zalman could say what he thought, and they might say something different, but all would nod, if not exactly in agreement, at least in peace.

The fourth tenant, Finkel, was a man Zalman avoided completely, after his first contacts some years before, when Zalman had first moved in. Finkel was, or rather had been, a lawyer. He still had an office downtown in a crumbling office building surrounded by expressways, ramps and urban renewal, which had driven out most of its occupants and would soon overwhelm the building itself. No matter, he hardly had any clients, so irascible and unreliable had he become.

I don't know that Finkel could have been called senile, but he certainly was unreasonable. He held confused and contradictory opinions on every subject, and was firm and vociferous in every statement. He never heard an opinion he didn't consider ridiculous. It was impossible even to agree with him. If, for peace, you said, "Yes, yes; you're perfectly right," he would say, "Ha! And you--look who's talking! You! What do *you* know about it?"

Finkel had come to America a Communist, before even the Revolution. Through the fall of Trotzky and the great purges he remained true to the cause, but when Molotov and von Ribbentrop shook hands in 1939 he came to the end of all belief. From then Finkel shook no man's hand; he lived out the rest of his life by negatives, for there was nothing positive to propose.

Above all things, Finkel hated religion, the opium of the people, the impossible magical dream of permanence in a universe he knew to be vain. Since his own dream had failed him, could he allow any other? Still--he dreamed just the same. He sat at his dining-room table in the half-dark, and read Pushkin, Gogol, Turgenev, while Zalman, downstairs, spoke his evening prayers.

They knew each other well, these two old men, strangers though they were. No use talking; each was the agent of the other's devil. For three years after their initial contact, until the incident of the mailbox, they addressed no word to each other.

****

Every weekday but Saturday Zalman would watch anxiously for the mailman, who brought his copy of *Der Tag,* published in New York. The mail also came on Saturday, with Friday's issue, but an hour one way or the other could do him no good or harm because he could not read it until sundown anyway.

Not that reading is forbidden on the Sabbath--far from it, reading and prayer are almost the only things permitted. Exactly here was the difficulty: what Zalman was forbidden, by close interpretation of the medieval rabbinical code he lived by, was the trip to the mailbox to collect his paper and bring it to his apartment. Within his own home he could, of course, do what work was necessary and appropriate to daily life--eat, dress, fold a tablecloth, take down a book from a high shelf. Outside the house--no.

The details are too much for me, but I have it from my father that it was impossible for Zalman to walk down the central stairway on the Sabbath to get *Der Tag* from his mailbox, because the stairway and front door were not his own home, but were public to the degree they also belonged to the other tenants of his house. Had Zalman been richer, owning a home in the suburbs like my father, he would have had no such problem; as it was, he waited each Saturday for sundown and the evening prayer before he could read the paper.

Naturally the idea came to him that he might buy the hallway and stairs and front door. In strict capitalist terms, of course, this 'purchase' would be meaningless. Indeed, he didn't even own his own apartment; he paid rent to some distant landlord. But for purposes of the Law, the apartment was his own property. He had legal, paid-for, exclusive right to it. How could he enjoy a similar right to the common part of his building?

By symbolic purchase. No landlord's approval would really be necessary, he reasoned, no Registrar of Deeds in the County Building, only a formal agreement between him and his neighbors, a verbal contract with a nominal exchange of coin, and of course his word that he would permit them to use his hallway whenever they liked. The logic was simple: the four tenants in their ensemble owned the whole building; together they could assign the common part to Zalman. He checked this out with his Rabbi, and explained it to my father enough times to convince himself the plan had no flaw.

With my father as witness, then, he contracted easily enough with Berman and Holtz. But how was he to convince Finkel? The problem was grave. Berman had already reported that Finkel, on hearing what was afoot, swore (or affirmed) that he would take part in no such exercise in superstition.

Weeks went by; Zalman talked to my father, on each Sunday visit, of nothing else. He demonstrated a hundred times the justice of his request and the unimportance to Finkel of nominal control of the stairway; but when my father said 'Zalman, don't tell me, tell Finkel,' Zalman fell silent. He had no plan, and justice alone is not enough. So finally, my father went himself to Finkel.

Now my father Jacob had (I think) no peer as a negotiator. Through the whole Depression, in his dry goods store, his receipts never equalled his costs; wit made up the difference. I saw him once argue a renewal of lease with the landlord of his store building. Birnbaum. The problem--and he solved it--was to obtain a reduction in rent on the grounds that it was to Birnbaum's economic interest. An incredible performance, with pencilled calculations and hours' worth of irrelevancies. First he exchanged part of the flat rental against a certain percentage of gross sales. Then he exchanged part of this percentage for Birnbaum's share of the heating bill. Then he reversed the payment of utilities against a rise in flat rental. Then, glowing with the promise of good business, he traded flat rental for another part of the gross. So it went in an endless circle, the prognosis of business receipts and winter temperatures ever shifting. Each time a formula was reached, he had some new idea which could not but enrich poor old Birnbaum (who had a heart condition and a dozen properties). When all was ended and signed, Birnbaum needed a lawyer to explain what had happened to him, and his doctor forbade him ever to talk to my father again. It's a fact; only my brother could deal with Birnbaum after that terrible day.

Even so, Finkel was not easy. I wish I could have been there. I suppose my father alternated advantages, his usual style, but what advantages? Perhaps he pointed out that if God did not exist, Finkel's refusal to sell the hallway was an empty gesture--even maybe a *religious* gesture. Maybe he offered Finkel a cash bribe, who knows? He didn't say. At the end of an hour he came downstairs to Zalman and said it was all decided. Then the two brothers went upstairs to complete the contract.

Finkel was sitting at his round dining-room table, in the half-dark, where my father had left him. Probably he was sorry already.

"O.K." he said impatiently, "So I sell you the hallway. Never mind the dime. Take the hallway and leave me alone."

But Zalman, though mild and quiet, knew what had to be done to make the contract valid. He spoke the words carefully.

"You agree to sell me, for one dime, your share in the hallway, stairs, and front door?"

"Yah."

"Yankele (this was my father)--you hear this?"

"Yes, he agrees."

"And, I agree to let you use the hallway, stairs and front door any time you like," said Zalman, "Yankele--you hear this?"

"Yes, I hear."

Then Zalman took out his handkerchief and laid it on the table. In Nasielsk, in the Rabbi's court (for Jews avoided the public courts), the grasping of the handkerchief had been the final seal of contract. It was the witness of God. Zalman waited quietly for Finkel to touch the handkerchief.

This Finkel had not seen for fifty years, since his own childhood in Mlawa. It must have called suddenly to his mind the world of that time: bearded Jews rocking in prayer, the hard wooden benches of his day-long schoolroom, where fidgeting was flogged, the hunger, the gloom, the superstition--all that he had escaped by walking, at the age of 12, from Mlawa to Danzig. He stowed away on a ship to New York, he starved, he labored, he went to night school. A brave new world he didn't quite find, but was he to return to this?

He stood up in anger. "No!" he was purple. "No! Get out of here with your black magic! Get out!"

There was nothing more to be done; some problems will never be resolved. My father's diplomacy might squeeze a dollar from even the most wary landlord, but what could it win from faith? Leibish Finkel and Zalman Reingewirtz, neighbors in their childhood and neighbors again in their old age; each had kept the faith to the last. It was not, after all, the hardest part of his fate that Zalman, for the two remaining years of his life, should have had to wait until sundown each Saturday to read Der Tag; nor was this the greatest injury visited upon the world by the idealism of the generations of Leibish Finkel.

Chapter IV: **Concerning the Law**

The Majority Opinion

To the Provost:

THE GRADUATE students who are the subject of this judgment were brought before us by the University administration for our recommendation as to disciplinary action. What was actually done on November 8, 1967 is well known; that these twenty-three students were among those who did it is not in dispute.

On that Wednesday at about 9:30 a.m. these students joined a number of other persons (at least a hundred) who sat down in a narrow corridor on the third floor of the Thoreau Building. They sat in such a way that virtually all the floor space leading to the Placement Office was covered with their bodies. Not long after they took up their positions, a fellow student named Walter Zukovsky attempted to traverse the corridor and enter the office.

He found that this could only be done by walking on the bodies of the sitters, and he complained to Joseph Rowe, Associate Provost, who was standing beside him. Mr. Rowe informed the students (and others) sitting there that their presence was not pursuant to valid University business, that they were preventing Mr. Zukovsky from conducting his business which was valid, and that if they did not disperse they would be violating Mr. Zukovsky's rights and would be subjecting themselves to disciplinary action by the University.

Mr. Rowe's request and warning were repeated. In addition, Mr. Rowe read aloud the statement of President McAdam and the November 2 resolution of the Faculty Senate (Appendices I and II). These resolutions made it plain that President McAdam and the Senate, who had been informed that such an obstruction was planned, considered the action intolerable, an interference with the freedom of the whole University, and therefore an offense against the community which would merit disciplinary action.

These students (and their fellows) continued their obstruction. Provost Rowe thereupon gathered as many of their signatures as they would give freely (admittedly not from everybody there) and explained that disciplinary action would follow.

A few minutes later Dr. Peterkin of the Dow Chemical Company attempted to leave the Placement Office, but found his egress blocked by the same group of students (and others). In his case, however, the passage was effected, though with some difficulty, by walking (in two or three instances) upon the bodies of some of the sitters. A few minutes after this the sitters got up and left the building.

There are three questions which this Committee must answer here:

1) Is the Graduate Committee of the College of Liberal Arts empowered by its charter to investigate Provost Rowe's complaint against these students, and to recommend disciplinary action if it feels it warranted?

2) If so, do we believe these students, or some of them, have in fact committed an offense against the University which does warrant disciplinary action?

3) If so, what shall that action be?

1) *Jurisdiction.* The law of the land is established by and enforced by the United States, the State of New York, Valparaiso County and the Town of Gunderson, so far as we here are concerned; how does it happen that this Committee shares in its exercise? The answer is, simply enough, that it does not. What we do or do not do cannot in any way be in abrogation of the public laws, or in place of them. We can have only such residual authority as the public law allows us by ignoring our activity. If we do, in fact, violate any part of the public law, those injured by us are free to appeal to the agents of that law for redress. Our own jurisdiction, such as it is, can only be relative to that internal code of the University which is a matter of indifference to the public law.

The President of the University is charged by the Trustees, who are the owners, as it were, of the corporation which this University is, with administration of the academic program and the maintenance of internal order for that purpose *(Regulations;* Appendix III). It goes without saying that he must do these things with due regard for the limitations placed upon him by the public law. But it is axiomatic and unchallenged that he has the duty of arranging procedures by which students, professors and others are admitted to the community, and by which, if their presence here does not serve its purpose, they may be called to account, or, if all else fails, expelled.

Many of these procedures have been codified; some have not. Thus we have an Undergraduate Judiciary which is hearing the case of the undergraduate students who were with these 23 in Thoreau Hall. It has a charter, rules of procedure and so on. Graduate Students, on the other hand, have had no court of their own, probably because they have not up to now indulged in the kind of student hi-jinks for which the Undergraduate Judiciary was initially formed.

Except for the undeniable residual authority of the President, no code seems to govern the disciplining of graduate students. Yet graduate students are very often separated from the University for academic failure. By long tradition such separations are initiated by the academic departments, which of course are best able to judge academic failure, but the actual dismissal is written by the Associate Dean for Graduate Studies for the good reason that this same Associate Dean is also *ex officio* Chairman of the College Committee on Graduate Studies. That Committee forms the policy by which graduate study is conducted, and it is the natural court of appeal if some question should arise.

At this moment such a question, though admittedly not academic, has arisen. It is therefore fitting that the President should come to us for advice, for if a code is to be written by precedent we are surely the body to begin the writing. We, the Graduate Committee, are the advisors the President should have in any case involving graduate student policy where a written code (apart from Presidential authority) is not yet available.

Thus in particular we are not a court. We consider dilatory any objection to our authority based on our lack of rules of procedure resembling the due process of the criminal courts. Such objections have been raised. The rules of procedure the objectors would have us imitate require a long history of litigation, an elaborate statute law and a specially educated corps of judges and lawyers. These cannot be arranged overnight.

We shall mention, just the same, that in the hearing we did hold the accused were acquainted with the charges against them, were present during the entire presentation of evidence, and were able to question all witnesses and to argue their cause. Neither Provost Rowe nor the defendants made use of a counsel to argue, but no evidence was suppressed and all voices were heard.

Another objection to the authority of this Graduate Committee depended on the assertion that we are not a 'jury of [their] peers', in that we are professors while they are students. That much may be true, but not the implication of consequent injustice. For one thing, we are not analogous to a jury at all, in the sense that criminal proceedings divide authority between a judge and a jury. In the present case the facts--which juries determine--are not at all in dispute. Our judgement is much more akin to the ruling of a judge than to the verdict of a jury, and even the common law (which we are not intending to imitate) does not ask a judge to be drawn from the peers of the accused.

What this objection really amounts to, legal analogies aside, is an accusation that a group of professors might not behave the same way, in judging this case, as a group of graduate students might. If the graduate student body were the only group affected by the events of November 8 a judgement by graduate students might show some advantage in 'fairness', outsiders having been thus excluded, but where the whole University is concerned it is surely more natural to turn to a group representative of the continuing interests of the whole University.

Indeed any 'court' could be attacked as unrepresentative in some way, but close questioning of the defendants has shown us that a court meeting their approval would probably have had to be chosen from their very number: 'jury of their peers' no doubt, but not in the sense of justice.

2) *Guilt.* Have these students committed an offense against the University meriting discipline by this Committee?

One does not have to argue very subtly to decide the answer is *yes;* and this is in fact our unanimous verdict. Dr. Josiah Willard Peterkin of the Dow Chemical Company was at the University just as his predecessors had been for thirty years or more, to interview students who were looking for a job. It has long been an accepted and recognized function of the University to facilitate such exchanges. We have therefore a Placement Office. In addition, all our professors are accustomed to write letters of recommendation for their students, thousands each year. Our bulletin boards are filled with announcements relating to employment opportunities.

It may be--as some argue--that we ought not to occupy University time and effort with student placement. This Committee did not feel compelled to decide this issue. We find that the attempted interview between Mr. Zukovsky and Dr. Peterkin did constitute, as of last November 8, valid, legitimate University business.

The sitting students were present in Thoreau for another purpose. One doesn't have to enquire into the purpose to decide whether Provost Rowe was entitled to ask them to disperse. Even if they had gathered there by accident, their density impeded the work of the Placement Office. When asked to leave they should have done so. Indeed, they could have been asked to leave because they constituted a hazard to themselves in case of fire, a hazard which the fire ordinances of the City of Gunderson require the University to avoid (Appendix IV).

Without judgment as to their purpose in being there, then, these twenty-three students stood in defiance of Mr. Rowe's legitimate demand that they disperse. If their purpose there had been a good one, they would still have been required to accomplish it in some manner which did not stop traffic.

However, we *do* know their purpose there. It was precisely, as they all agree, to make it impossible for Mr. Zukovsky's interview to take place except he walk on their bodies. As one of the twenty-three stated in testimony designed to prove that no real obstruction took place, "If he [Mr. Zukovsky] was so terribly anxious to get a job making napalm to burn little children, surely he wouldn't worry about stepping on a few of us!"

The Committee believes that the restricted choice offered Mr. Zukovsky by the sitters was an interference with his liberty. The sitters were not engaging in a legitimate University activity. They were not only not accidentally there, they were wrongly there, and wilfully so. They knew they were wrongly there because they were told so by the Associate Provost, and the President, and the Senate, both before and during their action. Their behavior therefore merits censure and disciplinary action.

Now let us consider the arguments raised, during the hearing, in defense of their act. These defenses sometimes overlap, and sometimes conflict with one another. This fact alone is of no detriment to the defense; conflicting defenses have long been a feature of legal proceedings. Besides, not every one of these defenses was raised by every one of the twenty-three. It is possible to assume, though we did not enquire too closely into the matter, that a student claiming one of these defenses did not simultaneously claim a conflicting one, the latter perhaps having been raised by some other defendant. We take them up here to deny them all, whoever raised which being therefore immaterial to our verdict.

(a) "Recruiting for jobs is not a legitimate University function."

To this argument the Committee replies merely that it *is*. The President has said it is, and since in so saying he is within our Charter as a University, and abrogating no law of the nation, state, county, or city, his announcement defines the legitimacy of the Placement Office.

What the University's business *ought* to be, or what it was ten years ago, or will be ten years hence, is another matter and not to the present purpose. Even so, the Committee was willing to entertain and to investigate the notion that placement ought not to be University business, if only to decide whether the defendants had perhaps some shred of moral justification (legal justification being out of the question).

We observed that the matter of what ought to be University business is a subject of constant debate and change. In this debate our twenty-three students have some voice, but only twenty-three voices out of thousands (this disregarding the unequal value of all these voices). The Placement Office has operated in its present manner for over thirty years, as has been noted, and representatives of any business or institution with a valid interest in interviewing, and a legal job to offer, have been fully accorded its aid. Until a week or two before November 8 not one of the twenty-three students questioned the validity of the operation, and indeed we have discovered that two of the twenty-three are actually on file, at their own request, with this very placement office, in order to provide certain agencies (though not the Dow Chemical Company) access to their academic records. Of course these two may not have been among those contesting the legitimacy of the Placement Office function. Even if they were, they might have changed their minds, and simply neglected to inform that Office. Yet however sincere their belief may be that the Placement Office ought to be abolished, they have certainly not taken what steps lay within their power and competence to urge its abolition, before they took the drastic step of physically hindering its operation.

The Committee has also ascertained that there is a considerable body of student and faculty opinion in favor of the operation of a Placement Office along present lines. We have not conducted a referendum, but neither have the twenty-three defendants. Even if a referendum were the proper mode of change, as some of the defendants allege--indeed, *whatever* method of forming policy is correct, legal or best--the imposition of change cannot possibly be the prerogative of twenty-three or a hundred students on a sudden Wednesday morning in November.

(b) "There was no obstruction, since the interview could have taken place had Mr. Zukovsky walked on a few people, and since in fact all the scheduled interviews did take place later on in another building."

The Committee regards this defense as a childish legalism. An obstruction need not be eternal in order to qualify as an obstruction. Ten minutes will do, and more than ten was accomplished here. As for walking on bodies--an obstruction need not be total in order to qualify as an obstruction. We conclude that Mr. Zukovsky who did not in fact traverse the hall, was obstructed, and the Dr. Peterkin, who did in fact succeed in passing the demonstrators by walking on them, was equally obstructed.

(c) "The obstruction was legal while the proposed Zukovsky-Peterkin interview was not, because the demonstration was designed to inhibit an attempted act of genocide, and genocide has been declared illegal by the Nuremberg trials and later by international treaty."

Here the Committee concedes that an action necessary to prevent a crime, if it be reasonably suited to the purpose, is not punishable. Thus a citizen has the right to restrain a would-be murderer by physical means which in other circumstances would be construed as an assault.

To credit this defense we would have to declare that

(i) The United States is engaged in genocide in Viet Nam;
(ii) The Dow Chemical Company is abetting the United States' purpose;
(iii) Dr. Peterkin is aiding the Dow Chemical Company in this abetting;
(iv) The interview with Mr. Zukovsky was pursuant to Dr. Peterkin's aid;
and (v) The sitting on the floor was a genuine hindrance to the Zukovsky-Peterkin interview, tending to thwart the the ultimate genocide.

For this defense to stand, all the above assertions would have to be proved. The Committee believes the argument breaks down at (i) and (v) both.

To deny (v) we may invoke the analogy of prevention of murder by 'assault'. True, there is no crime of assault if I strike the would-be murderer so as to prevent his raising the pistol to fire, or even if I run his car off the road while he is on some murderous errand. But if I break some windows in his house, or harass him with obscene phone calls, my defense fails; I am guilty of destruction of windows, or of nuisance, because my offenses were not in prevention of crime.

We find, then, that the hindrance to the Zukovsky-Peterkin interview was not in fact effective, or intended to be effective, in preventing an alleged act of genocide. To put it bluntly, we do not believe in the sincerity of that argument. In support of our skepticism we may mention the following exchange, which took place during our hearing.

When Mr. Zukovsky had done testifying before us, he received one last question from one of the defendants: "Did you, Mr. Zukovsky, at least *learn* something about our feeling about the war and your proposed part in it, as a result of the sit-in?" The defendant was trying to establish, in other words, that the demonstration was (partly) designed to educate Mr. Zukovsky, if not to stop him, concerning his proposed genocide, in the hope of preventing the crime.

Mr. Zukovsky replied that his name had been on the Bulletin Board for two solid weeks before the events of November 8, plainly designated as one of the persons signed up to interview Dr. Peterkin of the Dow Chemical Company. Anyone in the University, or outside it for that matter, interested in knowing who would be planning genocide on November 8 could find it out without even asking. Yet during those two weeks, he said, not one of the twenty-three defendants, or anyone else, had approached him by phone, mail, or in person, to seek to persuade him not to meet that appointment.

Mr. Zukovsky's reply was denied by none of the defendants. This Committee therefore concludes that the twenty-three students did not in fact attempt to use *any* legal method of forestalling the crime in prospect, let alone all possible methods, before resorting to the method they did employ, a method, moreover, not at all calculated in fact to hinder that crime in any real sense.

As for (i), this Committee was divided at first as to whether in fact genocide was being committed in Viet Nam. We sought to find this out. The Nuremberg trials being no longer in session, we wrote to a selection of the signatories of the anti-genocide convention of the United Nations, obtaining some various opinions, but in no case evidence that the Government represented had declared formally to the United Nations that genocide, within the provisions of the treaty, was in progress. This investigation having carried us rather far afield, and inconclusively, we decided to regard assertion (i) unproved at best, and we further decided that even if (i) were admitted the plain failure of (v) invalidated this particular defense.

It is worth adding that in this opinion the Committee is not being blindly legalistic. We recognize that there may indeed exist crimes which are not recognized to be crimes by any known tribunal of the moment. The analogy brought forward by some of the defendants was Nazi Germany in (say) 1938, a time when that country was officially sanctioning crimes against Jews and others for which there was recourse nowhere in the world. Would not a German citizen have been justified, at that time, in obstructing some Nazi official in the performance of his murderous duties?

Put thus simply, the answer must naturally be *yes,* but this does not yet imply that the obstruction of Mr. Zukovsky was justified, nor yet that it should be pardoned by this Committee, acting for the University. The exactness of the analogy needs looking into first. Who, in the Germany of 1938--even assuming Hitler's Nazi party corresponds to Johnson's Democratic Party--corresponds to Mr. Zukovsky? Certainly not Goering or Hess, indeed not any Nazi party of SS officer. The closest analogue would be some new-fledged chemist, looking for a job with I. G. Farben, a firm making munitions to be sure, but also making aspirin, rayon and the like. Any German who considered it proper, at that time, to inhibit the operation of all parts of such a company, would have considered it proper also to interfere with the local police, post-office and department stores. In other words, his sole purpose would really have been to tear down the ordinary daily fabric of his society, in order to replace it in time with another. Such a person would have to be called a revolutionary.

There may be something to be said for revolution under such circumstances. A successful revolution against Hitler in 1938 would surely have done this world a service. But our reading of history does not show that revolutions which accomplish anything worthwhile are in fact carried on in such a manner, by attacks on potential employees of chemical manufacturing companies and the like, though we must admit that all revolutions are attended by a certain amount of violence of some sort. But one can defend a revolution without defending all its excesses, too.

The real point in refining the analogy is to bring us back to the present, in the United States. The argument is that since revolutionary behavior was justified in 1938 Germany, the same behavior is justified in America today. With this the committee does not agree (with one exception; one member of the Committee does in fact favor a revolution, but dissents from the argument for the defense anyway, on the grounds that sitting in a hallway is a poor excuse for an insurrection). Whatever wrong our Government may be doing in our name is still rectifiable; they are still elected by the people and accountable to the people. If the people wish to change, they still have the power to do so within the law. It was not so in Germany.

But how if the American majority wills the crime of genocide? Then, it is argued, there will be no change.

But then, we reply, revolution will not help either. The evil of a majority can be countered only by the slow process of education and persuasion--and this was open to those twenty-three American students, though as Mr. Zukovsky pointed out they did not try it very vigorously. Or--the evil of a majority may be countered by battle from the outside, as with the émigré Germans and Central Europeans who came to America ultimately to defeat Hitler with a might no purely German minority *in situ* could ever have exercised.

In summary, then, this Committee does not grant the 'right of revolution' to these twenty-three students, nor can it even credit the argument that they were seriously interfering with the commission of some crime.

(d) The defense which seemed to generate the most sympathy in this Committee was in direct conflict with the previous argument. The sitters were not *really* obstructing an interview, the argument goes. They knew Dow Chemical would continue to hire enough engineers, and that the Viet Nam war would not be directly affected by a few minutes' delay in a rather unimportant interview. What they were really performing was a symbolic act, a symbolic obstruction, a symbolic defiance, the purpose of which was to educate the University community (not necessarily Mr. Zukovsky or Dr. Peterkin) to their point of view.

The defiance of Provost Rowe, they argue, was not a real defiance; indeed, they had talked over the whole procedure with him days before, in a friendly way (Not that Mr. Rowe had approved their intention). There was no real anarchy or revolution implicit in the demonstration. These students still consider themselves bound by valid University rules. The undergraduates among them appeared when summoned to the Student Judiciary; these twenty-three freely appeared in answer to our summons.

But, the argument goes on, these students are as much a part of the University as Mr. Rowe is, or President McAdam, or this Committee. Indeed, as graduate students they are themselves mostly teaching assistants, quasi-faculty. Three full faculty members were also in their ranks, for that matter (but are not defendants in the Graduate Committing hearing, of course).

They were, therefore, not just a group of subjects disobeying the Soveriegn; they share in sovereignty themselves. What happened at Thoreau was that two agencies of the same community--themselves and Provost Rowe--were at a certain time in conflict. Who should say *a priori* which of these two arms of the University was at that moment entitled to speak with the voice of the University? One cannot judge by legalistics. Perhaps the accident of American corporate structure makes Mr. Rowe the official voice of the Trustees--the 'owners'--but in the longer tradition of Universities the faculty and students are much, much more the genuine University than some administrative official. The judgment as to which voice is valid must be made according to the value of the two conflicting things these two agencies were trying to accomplish on November 8.

On the one hand, Mr. Rowe was trying to ensure that a certain unimportant bit of University business be carried out, business which was moreover quite outside the main University business of teaching and research. Valid maybe, at least legal, but surely not central.

On the other hand the demonstrators were attempting to perform an educational act of the first importance, a symbolic act of persuasion, of moral teaching.

These two University purposes, generated by two different arms of the University, turned out to be in conflict. Both could not occur together. But this is nothing new, the argument goes. When a classroom must be painted--a valid piece of University business--the class cannot be held there that day. This is then a certain inconvenience to another valid piece of University business. A barrier is put across the doorway, the students are forbidden entrance. Is this interference with their 'right of free movement'? Certainly not; one 'right' temporarily gives way to a more urgent need.

Similarly Mr. Zukovsky was only trivially deprived of access to a corridor where a rather large part of the genuine University was conducting an educational exercise of much greater importance.

This argument at first engaged our sympathy for several reasons. As professors, the members of this Committee tend to regard the faculty and students as more central to a University than its administrative officers. Even a hundred or so students, plus three faculty members, plainly constitute in some sense a population of more importance than the three who stood in opposition to them last November 8. If 'importance' thus measured were the criterion, the argument would win.

Again, a majority of the Committee happens to be of the opinion that the advertisement of opposition to current American action in Viet Nam is an extremely important activity, while a job interview between two persons in a remote Eastern town is quite a minor matter. If 'importance' thus measured were the criterion, the argument would win again.

Yet as we debated the point we discovered it is illusory to measure importance this way, and wrong thereby to forbid the activity judged of less importance.

First, the less important in fact often does validly take precendence over the more important. To invoke again the analogy of the painted classroom: which is more important, paint or education? Education, surely. Then one would never take a classroom out of service in order to paint it? Even the defendants didn't claim this; quite the opposite.

The truth is not that the more important of two activities always takes precedence, it is that the more important *more often* takes precedence, or that we devote a *larger part* of our resources to the more important activities, in proportion to the importance.

Hence the University has lecture halls and classrooms and offices and so on for educational purposes, and only a small corridor in

Thoreau for the Placement Service. This is just. What is not just is that educational services, because of their greater importance, should pre-empt *all* space, including that corridor in Thoreau.

Secondly, the opposition of a hundred odd students and professors to Zukovsky and Rowe is also a false oppostion. Not everyone to whom the events of November 8 were important was present there that day. The majority by which democratic decisions are arrived at is not at all the temporary majority of a group of persons who happen to be in one place for the moment. If such were majority rule, any man on a bus could be 'rightfully' taxed by the local majority and forced to give up his wallet to them. When such a thing happens, we are not entitled to argue that the forty thieves are more important than the one robbed man, even when he is a man of very small virtue.

It is for this reason that the nation, the state, the country and the city have constitutions and charters: to prescribe the manner by which the majority voice may be ascertained, in order to be sure that 'importance' is correctly assessed. These constitutions also assure rights to minorities, even to individuals, which majorities cannot overturn without very elaborate and deliberate processes of constitutional change.

This University also has a charter, drawn up in accordance with the rules established by the people of the State of New York. Until the people of our country or state declare our University charter invalid it is a democratic charter, even though it does not prescribe a 'democratic' government *within* the University. There is no conflict here. Our department stores and our hospitals, for example, are not democratic in the sense that policies are made by majority vote of everyone--patients, clerks, customers, doctors, vice-presidents--who happens to inhabit the establishment at a given time. But as a people, the citizens of this country do not consider themselves therefore subject to a tyrrany. We could some day change our rules for the government of hospitals and universities, but their present rules have our present approval.

Hence even if a sudden majority vote of the whole University had established that Mr. Zukovsky's interview should not be held, that vote would have been invalid, and Provose Rowe's view of what was on that day and in that place valid University business would have been entitled to prevail. But of course no such vote was ever taken; the 'voters' here were a small group of self-appointed legislators, creating a meaningless law in the framework of a non-existent constitution, and that law without any provision for minority rights, or the elementary right of free choice and movement of the individual. They were a kangaroo court.

In sum, therefore, this Committee has found no valid defense for the actions of these twenty-three students. They are guilty, as charged, of interference with the rights of a fellow student, and of a guest of the University, and guilty of wilfully disobeying the valid order of an authorized officer of the University.

We therefore recommend to the President that these students be censured and that they be placed on probation for a year's time. During this year any further offense against the University--when judged to be so by this Committee--will result in a recommendation of explulsion. Finally, we recommend that these students be forbidden the use of Thoreau Hall for any purpose whatever from this day forward.

(signed)
R. James Wendell, Chairman
Prof. of Political Science and
Assoc. Dean for Graduate Studies

Norris Koan
Professor of Mathematics

Bruce MacFarlane
Professor of Linguistics

Jose da Santo y Garcia
Professor of History

Jackson Robben Ball
Assoc. Professor of Biology

Julius Markus
Assoc. Professor of Economics

Concurring, but with separate Minority Reports:

John Francis Dattoria
Professor of Psychology

Johannes Bernardus Frobenius
Professor of Scandinavian Literatures

12 January 1968

Minority Opinions

(A) I DISAGREE with almost the entire philosophy of the Majority Report, but subscribe to the verdict of guilty and to the recommendation of penalty. The long justification of the legal authority of the Graduate Committee which begins that Report is quite unnecessary. It doesn't convince me, and it won't convince the defendants. The simple fact is that we were appointed to do the job, and that somebody has to accept responsibility for doing so. I would rather the defendants came to realize that our verdict is for their own good, than that they be convinced we were 'right' according to some code or tradition.

What these twenty-three students lack is a sufficient adjustment to permit them to operate effectively in a complex social situation requiring tact, flexibility and an awareness of the validity of opposing points of view. Punishment as such will not do them any good. I was glad to find a penalty (the placing of Thoreau as 'off-limits') which will remind them of the loss to themselves which in the real world is the natural consequence of anti-social actions.

Their behavior in Thoreau last November 8 resembled the sort of tantrum generated by an undisciplined child in public. He knows this behavior won't be tolerated at home, but in public he believes he will escape punishment because his father (or mother) will not wish to raise a visible scandal.

When such public behavior does in fact go ignored for such reasons, as is too often the case, he then has a handle on more freedom to behave so at home, for then he can demand consistency of his parents. Such children always put up various conflicting defenses, often of high moral tone, when called to account. To answer their legalisms with further legalisms is poor strategy, and only reinforces the original legalistic patterns. I regret, therefore, that the majority verdict fell prey to this trap.

These twenty-three students are simply out of order. They pretend to defy authoritarianism while themselves indulging in it just as they deny minority rights in the name of defending them. They must be stopped now, or they will be worse next time. I hope they learn.

John Francis Dattoria
Professor of Psychology

(B) These so-called students should be thrown out of here. They are not good. They are like the Nazis, who also laid down Nazi flags on the doorways of the classes of professors of 'inferior race', saying: "Yes, anybody can go to this lecture, but only if he is willing to walk on the sacred flag of the Mother Land."

Then when we ask them what defense they have for their action, they ask us: "What is more important, this lecture class or the soul of our great Nordic Civilization?"

It is disgusting, it has no place in a house of learning. I am sorry the Majority did not vote to expel all of them.

Johannes Bernardus Frobenius
Professor of Scandinavian Literatures

[The Appendices are omitted from this transcript but are filed in the Office of the Provost]

A Proposal Concerning Conscience

THE FIRST amendment to the Constitution of the United States is commonly taken to imply that the law has no interest in religion. Yet it is plain that this is not so. Many of our liberties, and restraints upon liberty, are formulated in laws which have no other possible origin than religion.

"Blue Laws" are an example: certain businesses may not be conducted on Sunday. Recently, noticing that for some sects--Jews, for example--Saturday and not Sunday is the Holy Sabbath, the law has in some places permitted the substitution to those whose consciences would otherwise hinder their prosperity. Atheists, however, who would conduct their business on both Sabbaths, are not permitted to do so, even if they swear (or affirm) that they will close up every Tuesday instead.

In this example it is clear that Christianity is the favored, historically prior, religion in this country, that other religions are generally treated as nearly equally as their voting strengths dictate, and that non-religion comes in a bad third. This is not to say that atheists get no consideration. A child with a note from home, in a tolerant suburban school district, may possibly avoid mention of God in his daily Pledge of Allegiance. But the general attitude of our society, and our law, is well expressed in the radio commercial that urges us to attend "the church or synagogue of [our] choice." To urge the virtue of non-attendance on conscientious atheists would sound as ridiculous as to claim tax-exemption for atheists' property.

The most striking current example of the advantage of religious conscience has to do with the Selective Service. Persons may be called "Conscientious Objectors," and need not serve in the military, if they adhere to a religion whose doctrine forbids such service. Persons whose objection to military service stems from a mere distaste for the task at hand enjoy no such immunity. They go to jail if they refuse to serve.

This distinction between religious objection to military service (or to doing business on Saturday) and ordinary objection on some other ground has led to a great controversy.

There are those who would divorce "conscience" from religion and who claim (say) a conscientious objection to war, without churchly authority. Indeed, they make such claims even when their objection is only to a particular war (generally the one in progress). How one is to distinguish such a conscientious objection from a mere well-reasoned political judgment, or moral judgment, is an issue the courts are now struggling with.

However, since conscience is the pratical equivalent of religion, in that both imply an inner moral code and a certain stance in the face of temporal power, I shall speak of them both under the heading of "religion." The problem we face is how to decide what is a valid religion. That is, as we have seen, no mere question for the academy. Daily life demands the answer. The law needs it, the army needs it, the tax-assessor needs it.

There appear to be only two ways to decide what a valid religion is: by authority and by self-proclamation. Either the law will name the genuine religions or individuals will be entitled to name their own. Each of these methods has insuperable difficulties, as will be seen; fortunately there is a third way, which I shall propose in conclusion.

First, authority. Whether the authority be democratic or tyrannical, it is demonstrable that none of our present sects would in its birth have received official sanction. Moses himself would have lost out to the worshippers of the Golden Calf, had an election been held on the day he was given the Commandments, while in most other cases--Jesus, Luther--the established church did its very best to stamp out the heretic. The religions of Moses, Jesus, and Luther are today recognized as valid under the law, but the authority of their own times held differently. To adhere to authority today, whether a decree of the President or a plebescite, would only validate those religions already established.

Today we tend to honor those great figures of the past who heeded their consciences and defied authority, but how shall we recognize those among us today who stand in a similar position? Even if we are not ourselves Protestants, we are taught in our schools to respect Luther for nailing his defiant theses to the Wittenberg church door. We recognize that Luther's conscience prevented his taking any other course, even to save his own life. We raise our hats to this disability of his.

So too, even if we are not Christians at all, we stand in awe before an El Greco painting of Jesus driving the money-changers from the

Temple. Money-changing may have been legal and authorized, and even necessary, as we very well know who have travelled abroad (to Jerusalem, say), but we still respect Jesus' conviction that God was offended at its happening in His own Temple. Jesus' conscience would simply not let him rest while they plied their golden trade. Jesus the mild and gentle was so stirred by the dictates of his own conscience that no law, no authority, no weight of custom, no man's argument could dissuade him. He was a Fury--you can see it in the paintings--driven by the force of conscience, a force impervious to mundane influence. He was, in short, in the grip of an irresistible impulse.

Naturally the authorities of his day brought him to trial and crucifixion. The laws of his day--both the Roman and the Hebrew--had made no provision for Conscientious Objectors. Even if they had, I think Jesus would not have been saved. His objection to money-changing in the Temple was not based on the teaching of any discernible Church; it was based on a very individual notion of morality.

Except for a handful of ragged followers, men and women despised and rejected like himself, Jesus had no Church. He preached from mountain tops and by the seashore, and not from any carved pulpit. A fair religious census taken over all Palestine would have yielded a certain number of pagan Romans, of Pharisees, of orthodox and not-so-orthodox Jews of various stripes, but it would have turned up too few Christians for notice.

America today has more followers of Timothy Leary's cult of LSD than Palestine had followers of Jesus; how could Palestine--let alone Rome--have taken such a thing seriously? Yet Rome was mistaken, as was seen only a few generations later. The self-proclaimed religion of the disciples of Jesus turned out to be a valid, legal religion, while the followers of Jupiter are no more.

If, then, it is legally important today that we distinguish the genuine religions from the frauds, shall we take a lesson from Jesus and permit Timothy Leary a conscientious immunity from our laws on the traffic in drugs? And perhaps excuse his followers from military service if they claim conscientious objection? In other words, shall we declare religions valid on their own proclamation, since authority is not trustworthy?

We *know* we can't do this, even though we are more enlightened than Pontius Pilate. The example of Leary alone is sufficient. However clearly we understand history, we know that to allow such a thing would immediately bring into existence a host of opportunists using the language of conscience to evade civic duty.

On the other hand, we know that to define a religion by what is traditional, or by census, demanding a minimal number of adherents, or the existence of stone churches and carved pulpits of such and such a minimal value, is also to exclude what might be genuine. Therefore we need some objective test for validity of religion and conscience.

I propose--at the risk of seeming a bit old-fashioned--something resembling the M'Naghton rule for insanity. It is well known that an insane man is incapable of committing a crime or of standing trial. He must know right from wrong, the nature of crime, the nature of the charges against him, before he is entitled to be brought to trial and hanged.

We have a corps of experts--psychiatrists--who are able to determine these things, and who advise our courts on the degree of mental incapacity of the prisoner. There is one test--among others--often applied which can serve as easily as a test for religion as it serves as a test for insanity:

"Was the prisoner, when he committed his offense, in the grip of an *irresistible impulse*?" A madman, that law argues, is one who has such impulses, not amenable to change by persuasion, by reason, by the example of others, by tradition, or by the letter of the law. His madness comes upon him, he is blinded, he does not recognize right from wrong, he is driven by an inner voice which tells him: Kill! Kill!

And so, naturally, we excuse him, and we hold him not guilty by reason of insanity.

I suggest that conscience too is such an irresistible inner voice. We can recognize a religious man by his conscience. He has a creed to which he must be faithful. He is, in other words, *committed.* Reason cannot change him; indeed, he resists, and will not even hear, blandishments to abjure his faith. He has closed his mind to logic, and he clings--whatever the evidence--to that prior immutable Truth which sustains him. He *will* not let Satan tempt him. And when he sees the path of righteousness, he sees it by an absolutely irresistible inner vision, which turns him into such a Fury (when necessary) as was Jesus in the Temple.

This intellectual disability we call conscience is, then, the touchstone of religious belief. Any psychiatrist should be able to recognize it. A person claiming immunity from ordinary law or civic duty by reason of conscience should therefore be tested by psychiatrists, at least three psychiatrists, I should think, and awarded a Certificate of Conscience if he proves his case. Presentation of such a certificate would then absolve him of military service, prosecution for possession of LSD, Sunday closing, or whatever his specific conscientious prohibition demanded. No one person, of course, is likely to be immune to *all* laws unless his conscience was proved very strong indeed.

I do not recommend that Certificates be awarded automatically to all members of the established religions, however convenient this may seem administratively. This would be innocence by association, as it were; no, each case should be judged on its merits. The man who proclaims adherence to an old code of conscience should have his day in court exactly as the man who proclaims his adherence to a new one.

Each candidate for a Certificate of Conscience should be able, when he does appear at his hearing, to present at least two documented and witnessed irrational acts, in evidence of his incapacity to resist his voice of conscience. His witnesses should be able to assert that these two acts can be explained on no other ground than that of conscience.

The Court, on the other hand, should hear argument from at least two men of reason, devil's advocates in effect, whose function it is to argue logical and plausible justification for the acts in question. The Court will then decide: If the candidate's behavior can be reasonably explained as deliberate, rational, the result of the ordinary processes of thought or calculation, the claim of religion must of course be denied. But if only an inner voice of conscience can be held operable, if the Candidate is proved to be so moral, so committed, so blind to persuasion that it is futile to expect him to live by the ordinary rules of society, then of course his claim to conscience merits general recognition.

"Actual Malice"

A SYNDICATED column of Paul Greenberg, as it appeared in the Rochester (NY) Democrat & Chronicle for April 28, 1979, carried the headline "Supreme Court Mindprobe Hastens 1984." This tag was probably the work of the local editor and not Mr. Greenberg, but it was not a bad summary of what the column said:

"The Supreme Court of the United States ruled last week that courts may inquire into an American's 'state of mind' when that American has written something others charge is libelous. The decision not only inquires into the mind, but boggles it.

"If taken seriously, Associate Justice Byron White's decision for the six-man majority would seem to be one of the few authorizations for a judicial probe of thought and belief since the Inquisition..."

The column goes on in the same vein, with words like "Rorschach test for witnesses," "Torquemada", "Nixonburger crowd," "1984", and "enormity" rather evenly sprinkled throughout, and it includes a particular attack on Mr. Justice Byron White as "Jack Kennedy's second biggest mistake (next to the Bay of Pigs)."

The decision referred to by Mr. Greenberg was in the case of Herbert *vs* Lando, the latest in a sequence of decisions widely characterized by the press as eroding the First Amendment; it was therefore more fully annotated in the press than most Supreme Court decisions. Two other recent 'press freedom' cases have been excoriated in similar terms. One was the case of New York Times reporter Farber, in which the Court ruled that a reporter must produce his confidential files if subpoenaed, and another was the case of the Stanford University *Daily,* where the Court ruled that the First Amendment gives press buildings and offices no immunity from searches for evidence of crime when the search is conducted under proper judicial warrant.

These three decisions and others were the basis for the keynote address before the American Newspaper Publishers Association on April 23, 1979, delivered by Allen H. Neuharth, President of the Association and of the Gannett Co., a large newspaper chain with home office in Rochester, New York. His lecture was partially reprinted in the

Rochester Democrat & Chronicle (a Gannett Co. newspaper) under the headline "'Imperial Judiciary' a danger to free press and public alike."

Referring to the Herbert *vs* Lando decision as a "chilling setback," Mr. Neuharth said "...The Supreme Court ruled that lawyers and police and judges may now rummage through our minds as well as our newsrooms...[The Herbert] decision clearly demonstrated that the judiciary of this nation is developing a state of mind that is above the law, even above the Constitution. This nation does not need or want rummaging of the minds of newspaper people. This nation does need an examination of the state of mind of the majority of members of the Burger Court."

The tone of both Mr. Neuharth and Mr. Greenberg suggests that in the *Herbert* decision the Court has newly applied a repressive doctrine subversive of the freedom of the press, in violation of the spirit of the framers of the Constitution. In fact, just the opposite has taken place--and that not due to the Burger Court, either, but due to the Warren Court of 1964 and 1967. It is ironic that the Court's efforts of the past fifteen years to enlarge the domain of immunity of the press are now being construed as a restriction. It is as if the newspaper folk were born yesterday, or at least since 1967.

To see what has happened one must review the recent history of the law of libel as it relates to the press. Such a review in fact serves as the introduction to Justice White's own most recent decision, so ably written that a journalist wishing to comment on the *Herbert* decision is better advised to read White and some of the earlier decisions there referred to than to go to any other source. Alas, most of the press commentary appears based instead on some textbook history of the Salem witchcraft trials combined with an assurance that the present Supreme Court is rehabilitating Cotton Mather.

Before 1964 the legal rules concerning libel (including slander and other sorts of defamation) took no particular account of the press, the First Amendment, or of public figures. Generally speaking, if one person published a false statement which defamed a second person, causing him harm, the second person could sue for damages just as if that first person had broken his windows. There was no need to prove malice or intent of any kind in either the libel or the window-breaking; it sufficed to show that one person--whatever his motive--had injured another, and then to settle the price.

The First Amendment was certainly not intended to protect libel. Anyone who understands the concerns of the authors of the Constitution knows that it was political discourse and debate that they mainly wished to protect, and that this of course included all other ideas, facts, and opinions as well: religious, scientific, philosophical, artistic. They meant Congress to keep away from prescribing orthodoxys, but they did not mean to allow people to injure one another with words.

For words can cause injury. Libel is one example. Crying "fire!" in a crowded theater is another. Conspiracies to commit crimes are punishable well before they have gone from words to action. Threats and harassment can be formed from words alone too, and so can the misrepresentation of a dangerous drug as a harmless candy.

Therefore it is simplistic to suppose the First Amendment means exactly what it seems to say: "Congress shall make no law abridging the freedom of speech...or of the press...," unless one bears in mind that "freedom of speech" does not mean freedom to say anything at any time and in any place.

At the time the Bill of Rights was adopted every state had a law against libel, nor was the Press exempted from liability for damages. The standards of proof required, the effect of malicious intent, the limits on liability, the distinction between civil and criminal libel, the notion of 'punitive damages'--all these differed from state to state, and like everything else in the law changed with time as well as place. But though the 19th Century was noted for its intemperate press, it was still no golden age of press freedom relative to libel.

In a Massachusetts Supreme Court case of 1893, Justice Oliver Wendell Holmes (dissenting, to be sure) went so far as to argue that even when the libel was plainly inadvertant, a mere misprint of a single initial in a name, by which error an unintended person was referred to as a criminal, the newspaper was still liable for the resulting damage to that person's reputation. Holmes' 1893 opinion did not become settled law until in 1909 he was able to write a majority decision to the same effect, and this time for the United States Supreme Court.

And as Holmes reviewed (in his Massachusetts decision) the history of the law of slander or libel in the English Common Law, it is plain that back to the very beginning libel had been regarded as a simple tort (i.e. a 'wrong'), an injury to be paid for, whatever the motive. In his 1909 decision, Holmes approvingly quoted Lord Mansfield (1774) as having written: "Whatever a man publishes, he publishes at his peril."

Now this sentiment did not completely cover the matter even in Holmes' time (or Mansfield's), as every lawyer knew. There are publications that cannot be held libelous however false and injurious they may be; they are called 'privileged'. For example, a sworn witness in a courtroom is free to say what he believes to be true--even if it turns out mistaken--without fear of suit for slander. Again, whatever a husband tells his wife is privileged against slander suits. A public official, such as a Congressman, enjoys an absolute privilege of this sort insofar as his utterance concerns matters lying within the outer perimeter of his official duties. And so on.

There are obvious reasons of public policy behind these privileges, some of which are statutory and some of which have roots deep in the history of the common law. The most important class of privileged defamations are the true ones. No matter how injurious the publication, and no matter how maliciously it is made, if it is true it is not actionable in civil law. (For curious historical reasons a true statement *can* be a 'criminal libel', but only rarely; this possibility will not concern us in what follows.)

The list of privileged publications is long and technical, but it is fair to say that before 1964 no libel was privileged just because it was made without malice and about a public official. As Holmes had put it in 1891,

"If one private citizen wrote to another that a high official had taken a bribe, no one would think good faith a sufficient answer to an action [i.e. lawsuit]. He stands no better, therefore, when he publishes his writing to the world through a newspaper, and the newspaper stands no better than the writer."

It would never have occurred to Holmes to privilege this particular libel on the grounds that it was spoken of a public official. Of what other sort of person *could* it have been spoken?

The general law of torts, of which libel is but one example, is filled with words such as 'malice', 'negligence', 'fraud', and 'intent'. Even where the infliction of the injury calls for payment regardless of intent, the amount of the payment may depend on it. Thus in most places an award (even for libel) will have two parts: ordinary damages and 'punitive damages'. The first is mere compensation for the wrong; the second is a sort of punishment for malice--to the advantage of the hurt party.

Now 'malice' and 'intent' have fairly obvious dictionary meanings, but they are very slippery to prove--or disprove--in a court of law.

In a letter to Holmes in 1880, the English jurist Frederick Pollock quoted with some pleasure a line he had just read somewhere: "The mind of man is not triable, for the devil himself knows not the mind of man." This reference was attached to the following comment (Pollock to Holmes):

"I quite agree with your thesis that legal negligence is not a state of mind, but falling short of an objective standard of conduct."

Holmes was at the time of this correspondence writing his classic work "The Common Law," and was working out his own doctrine of objective standards of fault, a doctrine that received its clearest form in a chapter precisely entitled "Fraud, Malice and Intent." It is futile, Holmes argued, to give these words their customary meanings in courts of law. If the devil himself cannot ascertain intent, how shall the jury?

The standard Holmes did propose as an alternative to mind-reading was one that prevailed for the long generation of his own service on the bench. 'Intent', he said, must be judged by an external standard of how the 'prudent man' or 'reasonable person' would be construed to have acted under the circumstances. If what was done would only have been done by a prudent man intentionally, then the man who actually did that thing must be judged to have done it intentionally too. So with 'maliciously'. Thus no mind reader, clergyman or psychiatrist is needed to probe the soul for 'malice'; one only has to look at what did happen, what was known, what was unknown, and how prudent men behave, to decide on legal intent, malice and so on.

In the case of libel, malice had always been a factor in the assessment of punitive damages, but it was also a factor in whether a statement was privileged or not. Some circumstances (like being on a witness stand) would privilege the speaker to utter libellous falsehoods only if without malice. The test of malice in libel, by Holmesian standards, would probably have run like this:

Did the writer (or speaker) know the statement was false? Or, failing this, did he publish it with reckless disregard of whether it was true or false? And, did he have every reason to know the statement was injurious, that is, that injury is the natural consequence of such a statement?

If the answers are yes, it is clear that a reasonable person would only have published the statement if he had malice in his heart. Given these answers, a jury is therefore entitled to conclude actual malice, without having actually to probe the mind of the libeller--except enough to find out just what he *knew* when he published. His mental *attitude* need not concern a Holmesian jury.

Despite all this, and the reverence generally accorded to at least the name of Holmes, the courts do not by any means always apply Holmesian tests. Malice continues to suggest 'ill-will', 'desire to harm' and other subjective qualities, and judges generally define malice in such terms when charging juries.

Holmes did not escape criticism from those who thought his objective standards were heartless, and took no account of the moral content of the law. After all, such critics argued, the law should punish immoral behavior, and immorality *is* a state of mind (or soul). Calling a man liable just because some innocent 'prudent man' in his place would have behaved better is to judge without compassion, to ignore the unique individuality of each case. And so on.

The difficulty with the compassionate view, however, is that it makes the law unpredictable. Who knows what a jury will see when it looks into a soul? Above all things, Holmes wanted predictability in the law. This too is a virtue, for without it every man's every act is perilous. Can a court really admit a plea such as "I signed it, but I didn't really mean it"? Without secure and objectively enforceable contracts, life is a jungle.

Acknowledging that "The law is the witness and external deposit of our moral life", and that "Its history is the history of the moral development of the race," Holmes still insisted throughout his career that the moral *phraseology* in which the law is written is a source of confusion and injustice if taken literally.

****

In 1964 the Warren Court loosened the law of libel, announcing a new Constitutional doctrine of privilege for the press under the First Amendment. The case was called the New York Times Co. *vs* Sullivan, and was regarded at the time as a great victory for liberalism and civil rights.

L. B. Sullivan, a Montgomery City, Alabama chief of police, had won a libel judgement in an Alabama court against The New York Times, which had published an advertisement paid for by a group of civil rights activists, Ralph Abernathy among them. The jury had found the advertisement false, and damaging to Sullivan. The Times appealed the judgement up to the Supreme Court of the USA, arguing that the First Amendment guaranteed freedom of press, and that if judgements of this sort were to be a constant threat, then newspaper criticism of public officials would become impossible. Therefore there should be a 'privilege' for the press, at least when it publishes in good faith, much as there is a privilege for honestly mistaken testimony in court.

The Supreme Court accepted the thesis in part--just enough to reverse the libel conviction. The privilege actually granted by the decision was heavily qualified. It said that if the person libelled was a public official (as Sullivan was), and if the libel was committed without 'actual malice', then the First Amendment privileged the publication and no claim for damages would be valid. The public interest was more importantly served by the extra freedom of speech and of the press thus obtained than it would be by protecting public officials from defamation.

The Court was unanimous in overturning the Alabama conviction, but as usual not unanimous in its reasoning. Justice Brennan, who wrote the majority opinion, was careful to limit the application of the new privilege to libels on public officials. He compared the libel law with the infamous sedition law of the late 18th century. Since that time sedition, which is more or less definable as a libel upon the government iteself, has been protected by the First Amendment; should the law be very different in the case of individual public officials? If the backbone of a democratic system is free debate on public issues, including the performance of public officials, does it make sense to privilege mistaken comments on government itself while not offering a similar privilege to good faith (but necessarily often mistaken) comments on the officials who serve as the governors? If million-dollar lawsuits are the price of free debate, is not the old common law of libel as Holmes construed it "a law abridging the freedom of speech, or of the press"--at least in the case of public officials--and therefore a violation of First Amendment rights?

Justice Brennan offered another argument based on the fact that

Sullivan was a public official. A public official has the right, within the outer perimeter of his duties, to libel an individual without fear of suit; why should not the reverse be true, at least in part? "It would give public servants an unjustified preference over the public they serve, if critics of public conduct did not have a fair amount of the immunity granted to the officials themselves," Brennan wrote.

The importance of Sullivan's public position as a factor in the decision was also emphasized by the fact that Sullivan had never even been named in the offending advertisement, which had spoken vaguely of "Southern violators of the Constitution". "They have arrested [Martin Luther King] seven times", "They have bombed his home", were two of the assertions, one mistaken and one true; but who were "they"? In another place the advertisement stated (falsely) that police had "ringed the campus with troops", and so on.

Sullivan had argued that since he was commissioner of public affairs, including supervision of the police, the false references were to himself. The Court disagreed, and this disagreement was part of the basis of the Court's decision; but Justice Brennan did point out that the idea that a criticism of "the police" could be construed as a libel on the police chief showed how unacceptably easy it would be to convert any public political debate into a libel case, unless some privilege were implied by the First Amendment.

Three of the nine Justices, while agreeing to overturn the libel conviction, wanted to press the privilege further then did Brennan, Warren, Stewart, White, Clark and Harlan.

Arthur Goldberg, joined by Douglas, wanted to make the privilege absolute, i.e. independent of the presence or absence of 'actual malice', provided the libel concerned a public official acting in his official capacity. Goldberg was painstaking, however, in reaffirming the general law of libel, and wrote, "the imposition of liability for *private* defamation [even of a public official] does *not* abridge freedom of speech..." (Emphases supplied)

Hugo Black, also joined by Douglas, said much the same thing, only in stronger terms, calling particular attention to the test for malice as a regrettable feature of the Court's decision, and rather downplaying the general virtue of a libel law apart from the privilege in the present case. Actually, while Black did not say so in this decision, he had serious reservations about the whole matter of libel, and in public speeches towards the end of his career leaned to the notion that "freedom of speech" really meant "freedom of speech", and that it should never be punished, however malicious or wrong-headed it might be.

The opinion by Black also contained a prescient comment. He objected to the qualification of the new privilege to exclude 'actual malice', in the presence of which libel would still be actionable, because " 'malice', even as defined by the Court, is an elusive, abstract concept, hard to prove and hard to disprove."

Recognizing this, Justice Brennan offered an explicit definition which the Court hoped might provide the desired objective test: To publish something with 'actual malice', he explained, was to publish it either knowing it was false, or with reckless disregard of whether or not it was false.

Thus a Holmesian definition of 'actual malice' was put in to sweeten the very non-Holmesian doctrine of a qualified privilege for press libels upon public officials. As it turned out, it was not enough. Tampering with one corner of a symmetric construction--such as the legal thought of Mr. Justice Holmes--may require more than a band-aid on the opposite corner to save the structure.

****

It is said that the Supreme Court tends to decide difficult cases on the narrowest possible grounds. If a case has many special features that nail down the decision, the rule of law by which that decision is made will be hard to distort to a new purpose, since the next case usually lacks one or another of those special features. Another reason for narrowing the grounds of a decision is to help secure general agreement, by making the decision not too different from what the Court had said in earlier decisions, and was comfortable with.

N.Y. Times *vs* Sullivan was not a difficult case, however. It was plain to everybody where justice lay. The *Times* had printed the advertisement innocently enough, as it prints many such political and activist advertisements, left-wing and right-wing both. The Abernathy group was quite right in its general charge that Southern authorities had been harrassing Martin Luther King and his movement, and in calling the attention of the public to the fact that Dr. King's very life was in danger. The specific allegations didn't name Sullivan at all, and while many of them were false or exaggerated it was hard to see that Sullivan had personally been damaged by them. In fact, Alabama law did not require him to prove damages at all, and it put no upper limit on what the jury could award.

Reversing the libel award was therefore a popular thing to do, and gave the Court an unusal opportunity to decide a case on grounds that were by no means narrow, even though there were plenty of special features cited in the decision. The principal basis of the decision was nothing less than the First Amendment. A new definition of 'malice' and a new privilege for the press (and not only the press, but all critics of government, as which of us is not?) swept into office on a wave of enthusiasm that was as much seen as a victory for Martin Luther King and civil rights for Negroes as it was seen a victory for the First Amendment. Motherhood would have come in a poor third that day.

As the years were to roll by, the details about Dr. King, the non-mentioning of Sullivan's name, the inequities of the Alabama law, the prejudices of its juries, libel privilege enjoyed *by* public officials, and all the other details that made the decision so easy, tended to get forgotten; and the one grand principle of the First Amendment protection for libel would turn out to be almost the only residue of N.Y. Times *vs* Sullivan.

The New York Times headlined its lead story on March 10, 1964, "High Court Curbs Public Officials in Libel Action." Some of the subheads were "Related to Race Issue" and "Bench Demands Proof of Malice". The editorial that day called it "a victory of the first importance...for the rights of a free press". Deep into the editorial was this comment.

"What the decision means is that in presenting the news or...in editorial-type advertisements, the freedom to criticize [public officials] is protected subject only to the reasonable limitation that the criticism be made in good faith and not maliciously."

Reasonable limitation? The New York Times had not yet gone as far as Mr. Justice Black. And did the Gannett press consider the limitation reasonable? The Rochester Democrat & Chronicle, of which Allen Neuharth was General Manager in 1964, gave the story small play when it came jout, but followed with an editorial the following Sunday, headed "Freedom Scores," which was mainly devoted to assuring the reader that the newspapers of the nation would, after this decision, surely honor their trust to be reponsible critics of government. The part of the editorial that characterized the NY Times decision itself did so in terms which made the result downright obvious:

"...public office is no place for a thin skin...a lower court made the award [to Sullivan] because of a newspaper advertisement that said unkind things about the police. To be libelous, the Supreme Court ruled, such criticism must show malice."

The reader given this summary may have wondered how 'unkind criticism'--even with malice--could ever have been construed as libel. Southern juries, one supposes.

The Rochester paper printed no noticeable reservations it may have had about the manner in which malice was to be discovered in court, nor did it complain that the complete exemption from libel advocated by Justice Black was not the majority decision. Indeed, of the four or five representative newspapers around the country whose editorial comment was quoted in the New York Times, only the San Francisco Examiner (Hearst) quotation referred favorably to Justice Black's position as the one the Court should have taken--but the Examiner went on to say "we accord [the decision] unreserved praise" anyway.

In the Sunday New York Times of that week there was also a commentary under the byline of Anthony Lewis, which contained the following sentence, perhaps unwittingly prescient: "It is true, as Justice Hugo L. Black said in his concurring opinion, that a Southern jury might find 'malice' and return a huge verdict whatever the facts. But Justice Brennan made clear that the [Supreme] Court will scrutinize any such verdict and put a heavy burden on the official to sustain it."

Mr. Lewis was still thinking in terms of Southerners and civil rights, nor could he foresee the extensions of thc 'actual malice' privilege the Court would make in its next decisions, but what he foresaw least of all was what any military man would have thought of immediately: if the defense (against accusation of libel) is improved, will the offense then rest content? In the present context, if the Court is to put a 'heavy burden' on the accuser, what will be that accuser's next move? As it turned out, it would be to shift the burden to the accused instead.

But there were some intervening years, during which N.Y. Times *vs* Sullivan had progeny, as the lawyers term those cases which extend or modify the rule of law laid down in the 'parent decision'. Sometimes the parent rule seems frighteningly vast, and the progeny serve to hedge it about with restrictions until its use is safe. With the rule granting the press license to commit libel absent 'actual malice' (i.e. knowing or reckless falsity) the opposite was the case. Within three years the rule had been extended in several directions, as well as confirmed by more routine repeated applications.

One routine application came up almost immediately in Garrison *v* Louisiana, decided 23 November 1964. Here the New York Times test (as the new definition of 'actual malice' and its use came to be known) was applied to criminal libel under a State law, and Justice Brennan, in addition to extending the doctrine to a technically wider class of cases, made it clear that the test was a hard one to pass (or to fail, according to the point of view). Though the lower court had concluded on the basis of the evidence that it was "inconceivable" that Garrison could have actually believed what he said about eight (eight!) local judges, Justice Brennan was able, without denying the inconceivability, to say this did not yet meet the test for "reckless disregard" of the truth or falsity of the libel.

If failure to believe what one says does not constitute reckless disregard of truth or falsity, what does? In St. Amant *v* Thompson (1968) Justice White gave the definitive answer. First he made clear what was *not* sufficient: Reckless conduct is *not* measured by "whether a reasonably prudent man would have published, or would have investigated before publishing."

Justice White, for a majority of six, agreed with the lower court that St. Amant, a candidate for sheriff, had gone on television with a story about his political opponent that was libellous, and that relied on the word of a single informant (though checking the story with others would have been very easy). Furthermore, it was agreed that St. Amant had given no consideration to whether his statement would be injurious, and had gone ahead "heedless of the consequences".

In the face of all this, White concluded that he had not passed the 'reckless disregard' test. To do so, the Court ruled, he would have to have had a "high awareness of the probable falsity" of what he had said. This phrase was taken from an earlier decision of Justice Brennan, where it had not been given much play. Now it was emphasized as somehow more reckless than failure to investigate combined with heedlessness of consequences. In fact, a later case (Gertz *v* Welch, 1974) made explicit the teaching the "mere failure to investigate" was a good deal short of "reckless disregard".

The case of St. Amant *v* Thompson, in addition to its linguistic differentiation between heedless and reckless, its philosophically difficult requirement of 'a high awareness of probable falsity' (four adjectives tortured into a single phrase), and its plain denial of the relevance of Holmes' reasonable man, also had the virture of giving another example to show that it was not only the press, but an individual, who could claim a privilege when libelling a public official.

Nor did the privilege long remain confined to libels upon public officials. Two more cases served to round out the domain of applicability of the new immunity, even while the definition of the immunity itself was being refined.

The first of these, Time, Inc. *vs* Hill, was decided on January 9, 1967, less than three years after N.Y. Times *vs* Sullivan, but a good eleven years after Mr. Hill began the lawsuit that the Supreme Court sent back for retrial that day.

Hill's suit was based on a New York statute headed "Right to Privacy", which made it illegal to use a person's name or picture for commercial purposes without his permission. Over the years the State courts had extended the use of that statute to cover other invasions of privacy via words or pictures, such as the publication of a false and embarrassing 'biography' of the prominent baseball player Warren Spahn (for commercial purposes, not news reporting). Thus the action brought by Hill was fairly close to a libel suit, yet did come under that New York law of privacy instead.

An episode in Hill's life had served as the inspiration for a novel and play called *The Desperate Hours.* The author never pretended that his fiction was the truth, nor did he use Hill's name, but in 1955 Time Magazine published a feature story representing the play as the actual Hill story and even including photographs of the Hill house where the incident had taken place, with the cast of *The Desperate Hours* depicting Hill's family.

Hill thereupon sued Time, Inc., and won a judgement which for technical reasons ran up and down the ladder of appeals a couple of times and ended up years later in Washington. Justice Brennan, speaking for the majority, reversed the judgement against Time, Inc. on the grounds of the N.Y. Times doctrine. True, this wasn't a libel case, and true, Mr. Hill was not a 'public official', but just the same Time, Inc.

could be held liable only if its story was a known falsehood or reckless of falsity. The theory was that Hill shared with public officials the property of being newsworthy, and that his privacy relative to the kidnapping that had put him in the news was already shattered. Only reckless falsity would be strong enough to negate Time's First Amendment right to print what it liked.

This seemed to be an extension of the N.Y. Times doctrine to absolutely anyone who was a matter of public interest, but in fact it wasn't. For one thing, Brennan had a very divided court. He secured his majority only (as usual) because Black and Douglas joined on their usual stand that even reckless or deliberate falsehood had 1st Amendment privilege.

Justice Fortas, Warren and Clark joined in dissent on the grounds that the trial judge and jury had actually met the Times standard, even though the judge's charge to the jury did not include the magic words "knowing or reckless falsehood". How could it? The N.Y. Times doctrine was years in the future when the actual trial had taken place. Fortas wrote, "...but a jury instruction is not abracadabra. It is not a magical incantation...formalistic codes recited by a trial judge to please appelate masters". To Justice Fortas and the two others the judge's formulation, which asked whether the article had "altered or changed the true facts" and thus "constituted substantially...a fictionalized version for trade purposes" was close enough. (The jury's answer had been yes, of course)

Not overtly expressed in Fortas' denunciation of the view taken by the majority "through the remote and distorting knothole of a distant appelate fence" was what seems to be an uneasiness with the formulation insisted on by Brennan for the majority. If they wanted to use the test of "knowing or reckless falsehood" as the only grounds for liability, it was because they were pressing, pressing--maybe under the prod of Black and Douglas on the other side--to make damage suits for libel, loss of privacy and the like, harder and harder to win. The three dissenters, along with Harlan, were clearly not anxious to provide an ever-wider scope for press irresponsibility, to the injury of individuals.

A year later, Justice Fortas as the only dissenter in St. Amant *v* Thompson wrote a furious denunciation of the majority attitude towards libel that he saw fast taking shape:

"The First Amendment is not so fragile that it requires us to immunize this kind of reckless, destructive invasion of the life even of public officials, heedless of their interests and sensitivities. The First Amendment is not a shelter for the character assassinator, whether his action is heedless and reckless or deliberate. The First Amendment does not require that we license shot-gun attacks on public officials in virtually unlimited open season. The occupation of public office-holder does not forfeit one's membership in the human race. The public official should be subject to severe scrutiny and free and open criticism. But if he is needlessly, heedlessly, falsely accused of crime he should have a remedy in law. N.Y. Times does not preclude this minimal standard of civilized living."

The other eight Justices disagreed with Fortas, who was not a great favorite of the press either.

The extension of the N.Y. Times test to privacy cases such as Time *v* Hill was, however, a bit off the main track, though it was illustrative of the lengths the Court majority was willing to go to widen the scope of the protection of the First Amendment. The decisive extensions of the doctrine, and the one that finally set the stage for the 1979 'mindprobing' controversy, also came in 1967, with the case of Curtis Publishing Co. *vs* Butts. Here the Court held (5 to 4) that if the person libelled is a 'public figure'--not necessarily a public *official*--he cannot recover damages unless he proves actual malice à la N.Y. Times test.

Actually there was a second case joined to the Butts suit, The Associated Press *vs* Edwin A. Walker. Not all the Justices agreed on the disposition of the two cases, and the grounds on which they agreed when they did agreee also differed.

Butts was a State College football coach who had been falsely accused of throwing football games. Though he was not technically a public employee, he came close. Walker, who had been accused of leading a riot and more, was a retired general and a political activist. This too came so close to public official that the extension of the New York Times rule to these 'public figures' did not tax logic by much.

In the case of Walker the Court was unanimous in reversing the libel judgement he had won; in the case of Butts they sustained it by 5 to 4. But of these five, only one (Chief Justice Warren) gave the New York Times rule as the reason. Just the same, there were five Justices in all who agreed that the N.Y. Times rule was as valid for public figures as for public officials, the difference being that of *those* five, only Warren felt that the judgement for Coach Butts was based on a trial meeting that standard.

The philosophical minority, Justices Harlan, Clark, Stewart and Fortas, argued that the arguments by which the New York Times rule had been originally sustained--that 'libel on public officials' was much like 'sedition' and should be more or less equally protected by the First Amendment--could not apply in the case of a football coach or retired general.

"Neither plaintiff has any position in government which would permit a recovery by him to be viewed as a vindication of governmental policy. Neither was entitled to a special privilege protecting his utterances against accountability in libel. We are prompted therefore to seek guidance from [other rules of liability, concerning] the improper performance of a legitimate activity by another."

The idea was that the press, somehow charged with the duty of writing about public figures, had bungled the job badly enough to cause damage to Butts that must be paid for. This comes close to Holmes' view of libel as a simple tort, without constitutional overtones. The precise test proposed was this: "a showing of highly unreasonable conduct constituting an extreme departure from the standards of investigation and reporting ordinarily adhered to by responsible publishers." This is quite a mouthful compared to 'actual malice' or 'reckless falsity', but probably easier to prove. It was this standard by which the libel judgement won by Coach Butts was upheld.

What makes this ungainly test interesting is that it illustrates one more time how anxious at least some members of the Supreme Court were to establish objective criteria of culpability. 'Unreasonable conduct' is not a state of mind, it is something that can be looked at with a camera, and only this sort of test can make the law predictable and to that degree just. Though Harlan, Clark, Stewart and Fortas were at the opposite end of this decision from Douglas and Black, who wanted no hindrance on the press 'right to publish' what it would, concerning matters of public interest, for any reason whatever, the bond that united them was still the teaching of Holmes as to the necessity of some external standard.

No matter, the N.Y. Times test won the day in principle, and from 1967 to the present has been the law of the land. One other notable case, that of Gertz *v* Welsh in 1974, arose between 1968 and 1979 to test the boundary of application of the rule. This was an attempt to extend the doctrine of First Amendment immunity (for a newspaper at least) to a libel of a person who was neither a public official nor a public figure. Gertz was a lawyer, who had got some publicity via a case he had been involved in, but was not otherwise public. The magazine that had been judged to have libelled him had argued that the case in question had been sufficiently notorious to bring Gertz into the public limelight, even if he hadn't been a public figure before; therefore the N.Y. Times standard should apply.

Justices Brennan, Blackmun and Douglas would have accepted this, but the majority sent it back. If mere momentary notoriety can turn a private citizen into the equivalent of a public figure, and thereby easier to libel with impunity, the press (which has the power of generating that very notoriety) might find itself under severe temptation. This was not quite the reasoning of the Court, which pointed out that a 'matter of public interest' is not enough to make everyone involved in it a 'public figure'. If that were so, the N.Y. Times rule might find itself applicable automatically to everyone mentioned in the press by virtue of that mention.

Though Gertz *v* Welch was something of a setback, the press had come a long way towards an absolute privilege against libel. In that same year the press also won the battle of Watergate and sent President Nixon into hiding. Its self-congratulation was comparable only to the annual festival of the Motion Picture Academy. Indeed, it began to look for a while as if the press was about to rise above its half-ironic title of "The Fourth Estate" and become instead the fourth branch of the federal government, with the advantage of not having to run for election.

In an article published in 1975--actually the text of a lecture he had given at the Yale Law School--Justice Potter Stewart presented a theory of 'freedom of the press' that must have charmed the press as much as the sight of his reflected divine aura must have pleased Caligula when he first became aware of it. The problem addressed by Mr. Stewart was this: Why had the authors of the First Amendment written "freedom of speech or of the press"? Wouldn't 'freedom of speech' alone have covered the ground if all they had meant was that an individual could also print what he had a right to say?

No, Stewart said, it meant more than that. He wrote,

"The Free Press guarantee is in essence a *structural* provision of the Constitution...Most of the other provisions in the Bill of Rights protect specific liberties...of individuals. **In contrast,** a Free Press clause extends protection to an institution. The publishing business is, in short, the only organized private business that is given explicit constitutional protection."

Indeed, Justice Black had said something like this back in his 1967 dissent in Curtis Publishing Co. *v* Butts, where he wanted the Court to "give the First Amendment its natural and obvious meaning by holding that a law which seriously menaces the very life of press freedom violates the First Amendment." The law he had in mind was of course libel, and the argument was that if, by claiming libel, individuals could so harass the press as to menace its life, then the libel law violates the First Amendment.

Justice Stewart thus carried this argument to its logical conclusion, which was to say that the First Amendment in effect *established* the press, much as the earlier parts of the Constitution had established the executive, legislative and judicial branches of government. Clearly so august a body must share the privileges held by the others, and in particular its privileged (even when false) utterances.

Such speculations may be the stuff of philosophical debate, but it was not long before this one appeared in a legal decision: the decision on Herbert *vs* Lando by the 2nd Circuit Court of Appeals, the decision which was later overturned by the Supreme Court on April 18, 1979, the anniversary of the midnight ride of Paul Revere.

From the clamor that went up from every newsroom in America the following day one would have thought the Supreme Court had repealed the whole Bill of Rights and Magna Carta besides. The April 19, 1979 issue of the New York Times made Herbert *vs* Lando a front page article, and the editorial attitude of the Times was well summarized by the headline "Newsmen Dealt Blow in Libel Suits as High Court Rules Against CBS."

The text of the story was however quite accurate, and the last paragraph pointed out that the decision here did not in any way change the law of libel from what it had been the preceding year. After all the applause granted the Court's earlier decisions, how did it happen that a mere reaffirmation of that law--in its every detail and definition--so infuriated the President of the Gannett chain of newspapers that he now sees an "imperial judiciary" where his own newspaper's editorial of March 10, 1964, commenting on the original formulation of that rule was headed "Freedom Scores."?

The answer lies in the fact that now for the first time the true fruits of flexible lawmaking were being tasted. The law of libel had been clear for centuries, and Holmes had made it plain that an injury by libel simply must be paid for. The decisions of 1964 and 1967 privileging certain libels published against public figures looked for a time as if they were saving the press from harassment and half-million dollar judgements, but there is another side to every controversy: the man libelled, in this case. For a few years, playing by the old rules and not yet absorbing the new, he had been losing his judgements at the Supreme Court level. But in the 12 years since N.Y. Times *vs* Sullivan he learned his lesson. If 'actual malice' was needed--by however careful a definition--then by golly he would get in there and *prove* actual malice. He'd tear the proof out of the very hide of the libeller.

****

Lt. Col. Herbert became widely known because of his accusations that the military brass engaged in a cover-up of certain massacres during the Vietnam war. Barry Lando was a newsman, a producer and editor for the "60 Minute" television series of documentary reports on CBS (Mike Wallace, the master of ceremonies of the show, is of course better known to the viewing public than is Mr. Lando). Lando produced a documentary on Col. Herbert that did not flatter Col. Herbert, to say the least. In addition, Lando published an article to the same effect in The Atlantic Monthly. Herbert then sued Lando for libel in the (federal) court of the Southern District of New York.

It is customary, much more so than it was before the present century, for much of the information that needs to be developed in a lawsuit to be 'discovered' in pre-trial proceedings, with the trial judge meeting both sides in a more or less informal manner in chambers--not the courtroom. Each side asks the other what sort of evidence is to be presented, so as to be able to prepare a rebuttal, and sometimes certain facts are 'stipulated' in advance of the trial, that is, agreed to by both sides so that no trial time need be wasted on testimony in that regard.

Of course, when one side presents a set of questions to the other side, the second party needs time to prepare answers, so that the pretrial discovery process in a complicated case may take a while. Over the course of a year, Lando answered discovery questions posed by Col. Herbert to the tune of 2903 pages of transcript plus 240 exhibits. However, he refused to answer questions of a certain sort, claiming a 1st Amendment privilege. Generally speaking, the questions he refused to answer dealt with his mental processes during the time he was preparing his material, and with editorial communications between him and Mike Wallace, and between him and the editors of the Atlantic Monthly, during this time.

The District Court ordered him to answer, so he appealed to the U.S. Court of Appeals and won. The Court of Appeals held that he *was* privileged in these matters. Herbert appealed to the Supreme Court, and the verdict was reversal and remand. The case therefore is now back in District Court.

Now a case appearing in the United States Supreme Court--by the permission of that Court--is not (except very rarely) a new case. Herbert *v* Lando had already been "decided"--twice--before it got there. The judges who had done the deciding were better acquainted with all the previous law on the subject at hand than almost anyone else in the world, and they were not stupid besides. Yet they split two and two on the question, for after the District Judge ordered Lando to answer all the questions, the Circuit Court ruled two to one in the other direction. **Nothing could illustrate better the fact that even knowledge, intelligence and good-will combined will not generate unanimity. From this one may form an easy judgement as to the validity of a free election where the vote is nearly 100% in one of two possible directions. Even a pollster on a street-corner with a clipboard is unlikely to obtain a score better than 2-1 in favor of the proposition that two plus two equals four.**

Judge Irving Kaufman turned down Lando's appeal on First Amendment grounds that didn't differ much in tone from things the Supreme Court majorities had said about the importance of the press in a democracy. He noted that even subpoenaed testimony could sometimes be refused by newsmen if it was irrelevant, and that that process of 'discovery' could and should be shut off if it were found an 'undue burden' on the other party. In one place, speaking of the 'chilling effect' of certain kinds of interference with the activities of the press, such as 'prior restraint' of publication, he said that questions about the mental state of a newsman, if allowed, could "chill...the very process of thought."

Judge Oakes concurred, but was more vehement yet in his defense of the putative libeller (Lando) in his role as a member of the press, and not just an ordinary person accused of libel. He reviewed the 1975 Yale lecture of Potter Stewart, and after speaking of the illegality of prior restraint of publication, an issue often in the news but not precisely before the Circuit Court in Herbert *v* Lando, he still likened that issue to the disclosure question at hand:

"The prior restraint cases...appear to be directed against the danger of self-censorship by the press arising from concern with subsequent executive, legislative or judicial scrutiny. It is the protection these cases afford that truly gives rise to the concept of the press as a Fourth Estate, coequal in our democratic republic in constitutional respect, even though not incorporated formally into our governmental system as a structural entity."

Judge Meskil in dissent wrote scornfully of "this fourth branch" of our government. As for the theory of Potter Stewart, Meskil noted that Stewart himself had held in a 1974 decision that the press had no special right of access to information not available to the public generally. Surely a "coequal" branch of government would! Meskil's dissent rested on the simple assertion that Rule 26(b) of the Federal Rules of Civil Procedure permits the discovery of any matter "relevant to the subject matter involved in the pending action." The trial judge considered the questions relevant in view of the heavy burden of proof now laid on any public figure seeking to recover damages for libel, and that was good enough for Judge Meskil.

Col. Herbert, by the way, had conceded that he was a 'public figure' in the sense of Curtis Publishing Co. *vs* Butts, so that the standard of proof he was held to required him to prove that Lando had libelled him 'with actual malice'. Having lost in Circuit Court, he appealed to the U.S. Supreme Court. It is the Supreme Court decision that the newspapers refer to when they say 'Herbert *v* Lando.'

The basis of the Court decision, written by Byron White, was the obvious one: If Herbert needed to prove 'actual malice' he was entitled to demand relevant testimony. Not only did he have the right to ask direct questions about whether Lando knew certain things were false, or had a 'high awareness of the probable falsity' of some statement he had made, but Herbert could ask about less directly related matters too: If a certain sequence, say, was deleted from the television program at a certain time during the editing, as a result of this or that conversation with this or that network or magazine official, such a fact might help establish whether or not Lando believed what he was saying in some neighboring segment of the program.

The decision of the Court was generally reported in the newspapers as 6 to 3. Paul Greenberg's column, which excoriated the decision as "one of the few authorizations for a judicial probe of thought and belief since the Inquisition," spoke of a six-man majority. As a probe of thought and belief, however, it was actually an eight-man majority, with the ninth man reserving comment.

True, White wrote for six: himself, Burger, Blackmun, Powell, Rehnquist and Stevens. Powell wrote a separate concurring opinion which cautioned against overriding the protection of the First Amendment too lightly, but which did agree that 'state of mind' and 'editorial process' were both fit subjects for discovery questioning.

Justice Brennan concurred as to 'mental state' but would have added some restrictions on the circumstances of 'editorial process' questions: He would forbid them *until* it was established that there had really been a libel. As another Justice pointed out, this would necessitate some sort of mini-trial about the existence of falsehood *before* discovery proceedings on the suit itself. What sort of discovery proceedings might *that* process entail? One can see infinite regress in the wings. At any rate, Justice Brennan was not dead-set against questions on editorial process, and not at all against questions on 'mental state'.

Justice Marshall too made explicit in his dissent that he regarded the questions as to mental state completely acceptable. His dissent was based on two other grounds. First, he said, the editorial process should be privileged, since the question was one of malice in Lando's mind alone. Second, he said, the very quantity of pretrial discovery going on in this case was plain harassment of Lando. The whole thing should be sent back to the trial judge and sifted for relevance.

This last point was the entire basis for Justice Potter Stewart's dissent. Stewart was the only one who didn't come out and say that mental processes are a fit subject of enquiry; he preferred to wait for the trial judge to throw most of those inquiries out on simple grounds of irrelevance. Then he would judge the remainder for First Amendment privilege.

Stewart in his opinion regretted that he had subscribed to the use of the phrase 'actual malice' in the original N.Y. Times *vs* Sullivan decision. Despite all the definitions given there, courts around the country were still regarding it as meaning 'ill-will, spite, hostility' and so on, and therefore allowing testimony that would merely be irrelevant if the standard were properly understood. He could not see that inquiry into the general editorial process was at all relevant to the New York Times standard 'reckless falsehood' that Herbert wanted to prove. The question is what Lando did say on television, not what Lando and his colleagues were saying to each other while preparing the broadcast and article, especially when they were talking about things that didn't even appear in the final product.

And, said Stewart, the First Amendment has nothing to do with it. Stewart, the lone real dissenter, the only man on the Court who voted as Mr. Neuharth and Mr. Greenberg and editorialists all over the country would have wanted the whole Court to vote, the inventor of the fourth branch of the federal government, was painstaking to divorce his reasoning from the First Amendment!

None of all this was noted by the Greenbergs and the Neuharths to whom (since they hadn't read the decisions carefully enough) Justices Brennan, Marshall and Stewart had been on the 'right side' of Herbert *vs* Lando. But even granting the understandable ignorance of pressmen with deadlines to meet, why should a decision that merely reconfirms what the New York Times in 1964 had called "the reasonable limitation that criticism be made in good faith and not maliciously" so infuriate them in 1979? Did they really wish an absolute privilege against libel suit?

Not in their words, at any rate. Anything that smacks of privilege is, after all, anathema to our democratic press. Ever since Richard Nixon's legalistic use of the word (in "Executive privilege") was converted by the press into *droit de seigneur* or worse, it has been impossible for a newspaper to claim anything resembling privilege, except in court, where, with a little good-will on all sides, the word itself might not make the headlines.

Indeed, I do not recall one single recent article favoring the recently increasing press immunity against libel suits, from 1964 to 1979, employing this word in connection with the New York Times test for actual malice. It certainly does not appear in the above-mentioned articles by Mr. Neuharth and by Mr. Greenberg. Instead, we read "liberation from a growing threat" and "shield against libel" in the 1964 New York Times, and "the right of every American to a free and unfettered press" in Mr. Neuharth's 1979 speech. It might be entertaining to scan the many recent columns protesting the Stanford *Daily* and the Farber cases to see how often 'privilege' occurs there too. The preferred word seems to be 'shield', with its overtones of knighthood and dedication.

Thus it seemed for a few years that the "reasonable limitation" imposed on "criticism" of a "public figure", that it be made "without actual malice", offered the public a fine, understandable collection of words enjoying the property of not for one minute suggesting a privilege for the press, while yet shielding the press against reprisal for its (not always 100% accurate) enthusiasms in behalf of the public it serves.

Then Colonel Herbert, equally enthusiastic in his use of the discovery procedure, found a way to make this "reasonable limitation" onerous. One of the mutants of The New York Times test replaced the external, or objective, test for 'actual malice' by a subjective gobbledygook: "High awareness of probable falsity." This new formula, designed to strengthen the shield of the press, in fact exposed a flank. Col. Herbert attacked.

Awareness, is it? *High* awareness? In that case, Col. Herbert had a few questions to ask, maybe a few thousand pages' worth. The trial judge, understanding awareness to be a state of mind, allowed the questions as relevant. Perhaps he smiled. But the Press smiled not; its steamroller had no intention of being stopped by a semantic oversight.

At the Circuit Court level, then, Judges Kaufman and Oakes were persuaded to formulate a new non-privilege for the press. Not only must "high awareness of probable falsity" be proved, but the man who wishes to prove it must also have one hand tied behind his back, i.e. be permitted no questions about 'state of mind', among other things.

The doctrine that "high awareness" is unrelated to one's state of mind was, for as long as it lasted, quite palatable to the press. There were no Gannett or New York Times denunciations of Judge Kaufman's decision. As for Judge Oakes' concurrence, including the proposition that the First Amendment intended the press to be a fourth, "coequal" branch of the Federal government--well, all in good time, on supposes.

The press was therefore looking forward in all sanguinity to the next stage in its appointment to high office by the Supreme Court when the April decision in Herbert *vs* Lando shattered the dream. In terms of strict law the verdict was no setback at all, except relative to the Circuit Court majority opinions, but in terms of disappointed expectations is it any wonder the result sounded like 1812, and was called 1984?

****

In his essay *On Experience,* Montaigne wrote, "When reason fails, we use experience." In granting priority to reason, Montaigne was actually only expressing piety towards his Scholastic predecessors, who had no use for experience at all. By the time of Holmes such delicacy was no longer necessary; on the first page of *The Common Law* we read, "The life of the law has not been logic; it has been experience."

In truth, experience is all there is, for logic itself is only a form of human behavior that experience tells us is sometimes useful. A Scholastic (and we still have them) may seriously believe that logic will enforce its own conclusions. Holmes, no Scholastic, in his essay *The Path of the Law* took another view:

"And the logical method and form flatter that longing for certainty and for repose which is in every human mind. But certainty generally is illusion, and repose is not the destiny of man."

We live in a world where people can be injured by words. These people want protection against libel. We live in a world where writers want to print what they see and think. These people want protection against interference with their work, which is also their joy.

There is no formula, no abracadabra of legal construction, that will forever settle the boundary between these desires. The law will forever shift, along with the desires of men, first to this side, then to that, according to some balance of forces that itself knows no repose. To some degree the law follows these forces, and to some degree it leads them. Men who study the law make a difference, but so do those who only live the results.

In the case of Herbert *v* Lando we have the most recent episode in a process that would not have surprised Holmes a bit, though he would have been horrified at some of the attendant reasoning and prose. Libel suits in harassment of newsmen were not very common in the 19th Century. DeToqueville remarked that one of the first things that struck him when he came to American was the extraordinary liberty of the press. He quoted a passage from a newspaper, accusing President Jackson of cheating, ruling by corruption, and so on. That Jackson should have sued the newspaper was merely unthinkable, and DeToqueville never even considered the possibility. He commented rather mildly that one result of all this liberty was that people didn't much believe what they read in newspapers. On the other hand, the ensemble of newspaper comment in the United States was so great and so lively that its contribution to civic spirit was an essential one.

Now if a public figure in the time of President Jackson were to have sued a newspaper for libel, something DeToqueville remarked was exceedingly rare, he could hardly have won anything by it. An honest jury, in view of this reputation of the press, could hardly judge that the libelled person had suffered damages if the papers were notorious liars and hence not believed by their readers.

In the past 150 years the press has grown more reliable, if less lively, so that printed or televised libel will not elicit the skepticism that met it in 1829. At the same time, juries in damage suits of all kinds have become increasingly solicitous of the injured person. This tendency has nothing to do with libel in particular; it is probably most noticeable in automobile injury cases and medical malpractice, and it is aggravated by the perception that the payment of any judgement will likely be made by a large impersonal organization, such as an insurance company.

Given these tendencies, and the fact that newspaper chains and television networks do often seem to the average juror to be infinitely wealthy, libel suits against the press are a more serious problem than they were even in Holmes' time, let alone DeToqueville's. Efforts to find an accomodation between those interested in freedom of speech and those injured by lies have evidently not yet been entirely successful. But these efforts have so far only been made through the courts. There may be other avenues.

We could return to the doctrine of Lord Mansfield, that a man publishes at his peril, and let the newspapers buy what libel insurance they need. The Court refused this approach, possibly for good reasons rooted in our culture but largely invisible to us now. At any rate, it seems unlikely that this generation will return to Mansfield and Holmes.

Another approach to 'libel insurance' would require legislation. Something akin to Workmen's Compensation might do the job, with the added virtue of granting the media the 'no-fault' dignity the present law requires them to fight for. We seem to be approaching this attitude with regard to medical malpractise and automobile injury.

It would be premature to say what will become of the conflicting claims of the future Herberts and Landos--it may not be insurance at all, or anything else now visible--but it is not likely that legal ingenuity and logic alone, acting on the materials of the common law and the Constitution, will give the answer.

One approach, however, surely deserves to fail, and that is the device of privilege that reached its brief apogee with the decision of Judges Kaufman and Oakes. The press is not a fourth branch of our government, and success in becoming such, even unofficially, would be a disaster for all liberty, including liberty of the press.

No mark of a totalitarian state is more telling than the fact that its press is an established branch of the government. One cannot listen to Radio Moscow for three days without thoroughly learning how the public's Right to Know is guaranteed by the Soviet Press, while the bourgeois press consistently violates this sacred, guaranteed-in-Helsinki, human right. But even in a democracy the danger of a guaranteed right-to-know must come to much the same thing, except that now it will be the Majority that will see that the right is properly protected, and responsibly served. Where there is a public trust there can be no substitute for public accountability. And this is the very opposite of liberty.

Do we wish to license news commentators? Make sure they have the proper college degrees, and have passed examinations set by those already members of their guild? Ask them to publish their financial holdings, to avoid conflict of interest? Require them to accept no favors from foreign governments? The list is endless, and familiar to anyone who has been confirmed by a Senate Committee. The press is mistaken if it thinks it can demand favors from the State, become an arm of the State, even a democratic State, and still not submit to this sort of thing.

Then let there be no more talk of the right to know, and of the sacred trust of the press. They both imply something ominously public, something to be guaranteed by the State. Let it be sufficient that the press merely be free, as I am, under the law that applies to all of us indifferently.

Chapter V: **Newspaper Columns, 900 Words Each, More or Less**

Magic

From Ambrose Bierce, *The Devil's Dictionary:*

Religion. A daughter of hope and fear...

Faith. Belief without evidence in what one is told by one who speaks without knowledge...

Magic. An art of converting superstition into coin. There are other arts serving the same high purpose...

Fine

THE BELIEF in magic never dies. I hardly have to mention the ones we are taught early in school to mock: the omens and auspices of antiquity, the tetragrammaton that conjured Mephistophales for Faust, the Happy Hunting Grounds. Which of us, reading of these things, did not feel a little bit superior?

Other magical forms carry more solemnity; we dare not laugh. Our ancestors were burned for less. Jesus raised Lazarus from the dead, and himself as well. Joseph predicted the seven lean years. These are from Western religions; others less well known to me certainly boast equally improbable events, and mandate rituals as bootless as any of ours.

A third sort of magic is having an increasing vogue on campuses these days. The Tarot cards and the *I Ching* have been around for a long time, but until recently Westerners who considered themselves literate didn't buy. I haven't seen many forked sticks for divining recently, or Ouija boards, but I am a provincial in Rochester, New York. The devotees of wheat germ and black strap molasses, and all the rest of the digestive intellectualism of the Haight-Ashbury of blessed memory, are out there somewhere, and some of them are surely wielding the Ouija board. Even here the legacy of the Berkeley street-intelligentsia is not dead, after all, despite the degeneration of the Haight into heroin and death. Consider Encounter Groups.

When one magic declines another arises. The flower children turned into street people and stormed the steps of the Pentagon, Columbia and Harvard. Like Joshua at Jericho they thought banners and trumpets carried by the pure of heart must win the day. Of course they ended up as disappointed as those who would cure cancer with prayer. The shrine may be hung about with many crutches, but the crutch shop back home is all the more prosperous. Neither believer, however often he must buy the same crutch, can thereby be persuaded of any fault in his philosophy.

The most powerful magic of my generation was psychoanalysis. This creed was typical of most forms of magic in that there was no way to determine whether or not it was working, and in that it cost a great deal of money. Of course it had a respected and well-dressed priesthood. Still has. Psychoanalysis is not buried, and may 'live' as long as Christianity, but I speak of it in past tense because its ability to mold men's actions is already only apparent. Christianity as a real intellectual influence collapsed under the attacks of Copernicus and Darwin. These days a religion dies more quickly. Miltown killed psychoanalysis after less than half a century. Mopping-up is to be done in both cases, of course, but the essence is gone.

There remains but one preeminent magic that I can see: Socialism. It is older than psychoanalysis but much more resiliant. Its priesthood is not particularly rich, at least in non-Socialist countries like ours, but it doesn't cower in catacombs even here. It is paid for writing in The New York Review of Books and for lecturing to undergraduates; it dresses well enough to keep warm.

As with Christianity, its mere failures will never be enough to destroy its power over those disposed to believe. Prayer failed for 1500 years before Copernicus; it was not failure that did the job. Similarly we must not look to Moscow or Havana to demonstrate that socialism produces neither wealth nor liberty. There are reasons, there are reasons. The prayer was not offered in purity of heart; Russians are used to tyrrany.

Something else will be needed, something that convinces with a logic beyond that of the academy, a logic that lodges in the soul. Like Galileo's telescope, like anaesthesia. I wish I could know what it will be.

da Capo al Fine.

The Triumph of Socialism

FOR TWO weeks in August, 1966, I went to Moscow to attend the International Congress of Mathematicians. My mother and father came along for the trip. They would see the sights and buy souvenirs while I went to the meetings.

My father had been in Russia 1920-1922 as a prisoner-of-war. He was in the Polish army in a little-remembered struggle. My mother, from the same Polish town, had never visited Russia. I myself was born in America, once my parents had rejoined here to begin their new life. Their youth had been filled with oppression, famine and war.

They opened a dry-goods store in Detroit in a neighborhood where Polish was spoken; we lived in a few rooms in the back. The business prospered for a while and they bought the building. They worked side by side every day, all day. There was no question of 'liberating' my mother so she could work; who was stopping her? She became--she is--a very astute businessman.

In 1933 times were hard. The banks closed, leaving my parents with $40 and the goods on the shelves. The City of Detroit, bankrupt, paid its own employees with a paper called 'scrip'; some merchants accepted it. We lost the building in 1935, but the scrip was repaid and we survived the depression.

From 9 a.m. to 9 p.m. my parents waited on trade, swept the floor and sidewalk, washed the windows, arranged displays, argued with wholesale salesmen, kept accounts, paid the taxes and brought up three children. Prosperity gradually returned, and by the fifties the business--now specialized to curtains and draperies--grew branches in the shopping centers, acquired managers, buyers, accountants; but my father and mother still went to their work six days a week and even seven. Not twelve hours of course--they are now, with the century, in their seventies--but every day, except vacations.

****

Two weeks in Moscow with their middle son the professor! We were pleased to find, in the main lobby of the Moscow University, that the Russians had provided a guide service, free of charge, staffed by Moscow University students who spoke foreign languages well. We drew Igor Korsakov, a student of Indian dialects, whose English was very fluent. He was delighted to take us anywhere. It was clear he had taken the job exactly to have the opportunity to talk with Americans.

Since my parents did not attend the conference they spent large amounts of time with Igor, though even I saw quite a bit of him. We argued about literature, Daniel and Sinyavsky, Trotsky, Socialist Realism. We gave him all the reading material we had brought with us, treasures like most of a Sunday *New York Times, Playboy,* Mailer's *Advertisements for Myself.* What a pity we hadn't brought more: *Dr. Zhivago,* say, or *Lolita,* which he couldn't obtain there, especially as he was a Komsomol member, and dutifully argued along Party lines in all our discussions. He took us to the monastary at Zagorsk, to concerts, to the zoo, and he escorted my mother to the shops.

She and Igor, she later told me, were walking on a busy street early one morning and saw a long line of people. What was this? Igor explained they were waiting for a certain jewelry store to open, where a shipment of wedding rings had just been received. Married people without rings naturally were anxious to get a chance to buy one. How did they know about the shipment, my mother asked, were there advertisements in the paper? No. Word just gets around. Igor was vague about it. People just knew.

They entered a clothing store, the object of their excursion. My mother had wanted to buy some of those typically Russian baggy shirts with a stripe up to its high collar, embroidered and all that, and Igor thought he knew of a place where one might get them. No use going to GOUM, the central department store, where the queues were three hours long.

Inside, the place was dim and dusty, high-ceilinged with a hint of pre-1917 splendour in the iron scrollwork on the balconies. The display cases were almost empty, dirty, inconveniently placed. The woman in charge of the shirt section was terribly busy over some paper or other, and kept her back to the new customers long beyond the time she became aware of their arrival.

My mother looked around. The store was even built with display windows facing the street, God knew why, since they were absolutely empty except for some dead and living flies. Without Igor she would never have known from the street what the shop sold, or even that it *was* a shop open for business.

"My goodness," said my mother, "If this were my store I could fix it up so that before I was done I would bring in every customer on the block."

"Why would you want that?" said Igor.

Letter From Vancouver B. C. (November 1, 1974)

(Written to the University of Rochester student newspaper, the *Campus-Times,* while the author was on leave of absence)

BY UNIVERSITY of Rochester standards my office here at the University of British Columbia is quite old-fashioned. There is no thermostat, and the windows can be opened. No ventilator or heater hisses, so that the happy sounds of the hallways come through clearly, even the sound of a mathematical voice from a classroom farther down. My desk and bookcase are made of wood.

The U.B.C. is quite large--2000 enrolled in 1st year calculus--and it is a state school, yet the student newspaper, called *The Ubyssey,* very much resembles the *Campus-Times.* It even printed a letter from me, with a heated rejoinder signed by the entire staff of *The Ubyssey.*

The controversy was (naturally) about the price and quality of the food service here. There is no "board plan," but the isolation of the U.B.C. from town is something like that of the U.R. so that students are at the mercy of the school cafeterias. The paper made a survey, finding that the prices are higher and the food worse than in nearby Vancouver commercial coffee shops and restaurants, and the gap is widening. An *Ubyssey* editorial expressed indignation, saying that the difference is especially indefensible when you consider that the commercial establishments "have to make a profit." By this the editorialist obviously meant that "profit" was a cost to a commercial establishment which did not have to be met by the government-operated cafeterias on campus.

I sympathized with the students, in my letter. Indeed, I had myself compared the prices and the quality and the newspaper was absolutely right. But that part about the "profit" got an objection from me. Had *The Ubyssey* never given thought to the possibility that "having to make a profit" was the *cause* of the superior performance of the commercial restaurants?

In the course of the printed commentaries of the preceding couple of weeks, in fact, it had been brought out that the U.B.C. cafeterias had professional dieticians on the payroll, something quite unknown, I should think in unhappy Chinatown. Curiously enough, most Vancouver citizens when given their choice will prefer Chinatown to the U.B.C. campus when they want a quick lunch and are in the neighborhood. And the only reason anyone can see for the Chinaman not employing a dietician is his greed for profit, something the U.B.C. cafeterias are free of.

I didn't get to say quite all this in my letter, especially the part about the Chinese which might have been interpreted by the editors as a slur upon an ethnic group, but I did say enough to elicit an angry reply accusing me of using the long-discredited argument "if its government-run it can't be any good." They stuck to their original recommendation, which is now in fact being carried out: a full-scale Investigation and Report by a Committee appointed by the directors of the University (who are public officials).

If they fire the dieticians I'll eat my shirt.

Up to now the U.B.C. hasn't passed a law saying students *have* to eat U.B.C. cafeteria food. In this they are somewhat behind the socialist government of British Columbia--at least with respect to alcoholic drink. Beer, wine and liquor can only be bought in government stores. The guidebooks to Vancouver all tell you how to find them, so it's really not hard, and if you find one you find them all since they are identical.

Henner's liquor store on Chili Avenue in Rochester has (at least) twenty times the variety of wine the B.C. stores have though, I am sure the public servants who choose the selection here are trying their best to please the average citizen.

Vancouver has a large Greek population, or anyhow large enough to provide at least five excellent Greek restaurants with authentic souvlakia, pitta, olives and so on, but there is not one drop of Greek wine (except a single brand of retsina) to be had in the wine shops and consequently in the restaurants. The provincial government does provide one modest Bulgarian red wine. I suppose that's close enough for democratic purposes; the Greeks don't have many votes.

The latest word from the B.C. wine board is that they have stopped ordering all South African wines. This was announced proudly just yesterday, United Nations Day, as a gesture of solidarity with the General Assembly which has censured South Africa for its racist policies. It is likely that a majority here drinks no wine at all. If the majority taste were binding on everyone in all matters pertaining to wine, the Greeks would all drink beer.

In the matter of liquor, *The Ubyssey* editorialist does not have the option of comparing government stores with commercial outfits who have to make a profit; the latter are outlawed. We'll never know which would be more efficient. There is nothing a Commission can learn by making a comparison. When the B.C. government extends its attention to food, we will be spared much controversy.

But I will be back in the States by then. I'll miss the foghorn off Point Gray, the mountains, the spacious old math building and many of the pleasant people here. I shall toast them from afar, when I think of it, in a bottle of Demestica white. λχμ!

Minimum Wages

A FEW years ago it was brought to my attention by some economist friends at the University of Rochester School of Management that the principal effect of minimum wage laws was to cause unemployment. Not cure it, not raise standards of living, but *cause* unemployment.

The reasoning is so simple that it is hard to get anyone to believe it: If the job you do isn't worth the minimum wage required by law, nobody will pay you to do it. And the sad truth is that lots of jobs have so little commercial value that nobody does in fact pay the minimum wage for it, and they are simply not done, while those who could do them are wasted.

If a man fishes all day and catches one small carp, shall I pay him $15 for it because he worked so and so many hours? This is in effect what the law demands, once I am called an employer and he is called a wage-slave.

Well, his case is not unique. Consider all the artists in the world, and the actors and musicians. The tradition of starving artists in garrets is an old and romantic one, and deserved. For each Van Gogh there were 1,000 wasters of paint and canvas. To pay them all a living minimum wage would have bankrupted Europe.

Well, nobody advocates that, you say. Think again, I say. The clamor for "government support of the Arts" is in fact nothing more or less than the desire to tax all of us to pay artists at a rate none of us dreams of paying freely by the piece or by the performance.

They can go on welfare while sitting for weeks in agents' offices, but the minute they carry a spear on stage they gotta get that "living wage." Worse, they get what Actor's Equity, the actors' union, considers a fair minimum; and Equity enforces its law on wages better than New York State can enforce laws against murder, I assure you. The result is obvious unemployment, $10 theater tickets and taxes "to support the arts."

All these old thoughts converged when I read recently that WBFB had fired four volunteers who had been running interesting Sunday programs on that good-music station, without pay. They had to be fired because the Wages and Hours Division of the U.S. Department of Labor had discovered their zero salary to be less than the legal minimum wage.

Fortunately these four volunteers were not starving; they have jobs or money elsewhere. Losing their WBFB jobs didn't throw them on unemployment insurance or welfare, as it might have if they had been the sort of people the minimum wage law is designed to "protect", and had lost some low-paying job they needed.

But the government doesn't draw such fine distinctions; everybody gets the benefit of the minimum wage law whether he likes it or not. Nor does the law permit me to hire a man to rake leaves for $1 an hour, even though he has the hour to spare and wants the dollar, and I don't feel like paying more.

Please don't tell me I should pay more; there is still enough liberty around so that I don't have to hire him at all, though I may be called blood-sucker for raking my own leaves.

The final evil of all this is not, in fact, strictly economic. It is our loss of liberty. At one extreme I can't hire a leaf-raker at a price I can afford and he wants to take. At the other extreme, four cultured citizens are forbidden to conduct interesting radio programs at cost WBFB can recover commercially through advertising. The kindly efforts of government have backfired again.

In downtown Rochester we have tax-paid officials in Federal buildings, consuming paper, telephones and heating fuel, enforcing these things, and who, every man-Jack of them, gets paid better than minimum wage. It would be educational for every citizen to go down once in a while to look at them all, and to take the kids there once in a while, instead of to the zoo or the firehouse.

It is a pity, in a way, that school children are so often taken to see the obviously useful government-supplied services, the police, the museums, the firemen; and so seldom taken to see the rest. Do it yourself. Take your own 10-year old to the Wages and Hours Division of the U.S. Department of Labor, and let him learn what they have done for music and liberty in Rochester.

The Middleman

VERY OFTEN the newspapers report that the price of groceries is up while the prices received by the farmers are down. The explanation (inevitably) is that "the middleman" is gobbling up the difference, and more. The implication then is that "something ought to be done" about it--price control, perhaps, or excess-profit taxes--something, at any rate, between jaw-boning and socialism.

But the middleman is a complicated beast. He is not just a cigar-smoking fatso with money-bags. He is a truck driver, a truck, a railroad, a health inspector, a marketing cooperative, a bank, a trader in soybean futures, a grocery clerk and a paper-bag manufacturer, to name a few, and don't forget the tax collector.

Alas, the "middleman" in most people's minds, when the word is bandied about, is the wholesale or retail merchant of food. A&P, perhaps, with the owner of a Chicago stockyard somewhere dimly in the background.

There is a long sequence of operations needed to extract a tender ham for our table from what was a snorting pig way out in Iowa. If there is any waste, any useless payment in all this process, that waste is not to be found in the merchandizing, which is in fact almost the only part of the process that is not subsidized or protected in some way from the free force of the marketplace.

Anyone can play; there is no limitation on entering the food trade. In this it differs from law, medicine, teaching, taxi-driving, bricklaying and liquor and eyeglass selling, for example--things which require either certification, apprenticeship, guild membership or higher education, or licenses from governments, unions, or protective associations--and all of which have the goal of "a fair return," which is to say a rigged system of prices.

Being a merchant is free and open to all; it is just the opposite of a protected trade or profession. It has no rigged pricing, no guaranteed profits, no building codes, taxi medallions or sick pay. If food retailing were the rip-off its more mindless critics imply, it would, unlike the protected and licensed and unionized professions and trades where this is impossible, be invaded tomorrow by a thousand greedy prospectors.

Why haven't we seen this gold rush; why haven't all our street corners filled up with new grocers coining money? Liberty is dangerous, that's why; few will risk it.

The average hourly-rated employee of the New York subway gets over $15,000 a year (The New York Times, April 6, 1975) protected by an ironclad union contract making it illegal for anyone to compete with him at a lower price. Should such a person, once he is in solid, expose himself again to the open market? Yet he is more free to do that than the retailer is to enter *his* world.

That subway worker can become a "profiteer" tomorrow. He need not bid for a medallion, work for a diploma, beg for an apprenticeship, claim minority status, pass a Civil Service exam, prove himself no felon, win an election or join a union. But he can be sure of one thing: if he does go into business and succeeds in making a living, he will be reviled by many a decent citizen who ought rather to wonder what happened to 1965's 15-cent subway fare.

I'll admit there is sometimes in the press a certain sympathy expressed for the "momma and poppa store" (as if Wegman's and the A&P were shamefully childless.) But this printed sympathy didn't do much good on Joseph Avenue, or in the ghettos of Newark and Detroit in the time of the long hot summers. The poor folk rose up against just those small merchants in their neighborhoods, the middlemen who (they had been persuaded) were the instruments of their poverty. What a mistake! They began with a ghetto and ended with a desert. The "middleman" was destroyed. Hurrah.

The subway worker well knows he is best advised to stay with the subway. What are profits to him? Only wickedness. So the subway has ever-increasing fares and ever-fewer riders? Then let the city, state and federal governments subsidize the ever-growing deficit--and pay his inviolate wage--while he complains of the price of food.

I despair of ever seeing a reversal of this attitude towards trade. In the socialist world it is of course an article of faith, and in our world it comes close. Yet however hopelessly, I shall here ask one small favor of the media and the public--even, if you will, of the Rochester Democrat & Chronicle:

If the "middleman" is bound to be the object of derision, scorn, contempt, anger and obloquy, can you at least have the decency to use the word "middleperson" instead?

Name Discrimination

PART OF the revolution is over; the first battle has been won. "Chairperson" has almost unanimously displaced "Chairman" as the description of the director (or directress?) of a meeting. "Letter-carrier" is to be used instead of "mailman", "Gerperson" in place of "German" and so on. Good. We do not wish to ascribe sexual specificity to certain occupations or positions in society.

Yet while part of the problem of sexual discrimination has been settled we must not think it is all settled. Not by a long shot, no sirree (or madam), not even in the linguistic domain.

Certain first names in our English language are exclusively given to boy-children, names like Robert and Jerome. Other names are only held by girl-children, names like Margaret and Josephine. There is also a third kind of name that seems to be indifferent to sex: Dale, Evelyn, Gail--but these are relatively few.

The existence of names with a definite sexual ascription perpetuates an unhealthy tradition, the same tradition that we have only partly eradicated with the abolition of the male-only type of common noun, as mentioned above. What good does it do to call someone a chairperson when in the next breath you find that the chairperson in question is named Cynthia or Thomas? The secret is given away immediately.

Surely a person should be judged by merit alone, and not by a *presumed* merit related to the hearer's interpretation of the name involved. Suppose--in a newspaper story, or a job application--a person's actions are being described, or the person's history. Wouldn't it be unjust to prejudice the reader by a premature disclosure of sex? Especially when we know that sex has nothing to do with the merits of the case.

There are those who pretend to adhere to this point of view, but who slyly inject the name of the individual (or person) to be judged as if there were no way out of doing so. They will say, for example, "I have just the person for the job you have open,"--notice how they say 'person'--"a person of impeccable qualifications, experience, intelligence, a person cooperative in every way and who will work at almost any wage."

"Yeah?" you reply, "What person do you have in mind?"

"Well," he says, "if you must know, it's Gwendolyn Josephine Schultz."

Now at this point you probably recognize it's a woman. This practice of surreptitious discriminatory identification by proper name can hardly be outlawed, because a name is a name and cannot be simply neutered by substitution, the way 'man' is turned to 'person' in words like 'chairman' or 'penmanship'.

But difficulties exist only to be overcome. A nation that has put persons on the moon can certainly solve this one. Several approaches seem possible.

We could simply outlaw sexually distinguished names, like Jerome and Josephine, and compel everyone to use names like Dale, which suggest neither sex, or to invent new names like Udrid or Quartile, which--never having been used for anyone up to now--start out quite neutrally.

This approach is quite limiting, however, and will not permit us to honor our ancestors, our heros, our saints and biblical characters as we now do when we name our children.

A better approach would be to use the names we now use, but to make sure they are given equally to boys and girls. If, over the course of a generation, half (more or less) of the Roberts are girls and half the Cynthias boys, there will be no more chance of distinguishing sex by name than there now is of determining the sex of a chairperson by that designation alone.

There are great educational advantages to random sex assignments of names. These days, children read about the heros of the past, Ludwig van Beethoven, George Washington, Ted Williams, Thomas Edison, and recognize by their names that these people were all males. By the time schooling is over, our children have discovered--without anyone's having explicitly mentioned it--that *all* our presidents, *all* our chess champions, *all* our baseball heros, and practically all our scientists, mathematicians, musical composers and inventors were men. This generates in the mind of the impressionable girl the notion that women are somehow inferior, and the lack of courage or lack of self-confidence that comes from this notion perpetuates the problem.

Once a genuine name reform takes hold, and children in school see that George, Ludwig, Thomas, Isaac and Ted are names as common among girls in their classes as among boys, they will read history with different eyes. 'Isaac Newton' will suggest a science person, not a man especially, the way the name 'Isaac' does now. Any boy or girl can be born with the name Isaac; therefore any girl as well as any boy will feel entitled to aspire to grow up to be another Newton.

The psychological difference this reform will effect is so enormous that I am suggesting it to my congressperson in the form of a piece of draft legislation. Not being a lawyer, I have not been able to write it up with all the p's and q's dotted and all, but the general idea goes like this:

Every parent shall be required by law to name any child born on or after 12:01 a.m. January 1, 1977 with either a sexually-indifferent name (list attached--names like Dale, etc.), or to use a sexually-specific name *provided* that of the total number of sexually-specifically-named children in a given family, no more than half may be named according to the pre-1977 "correct" specificity.

Well--the legal language gets kind of tough, so I won't repeat it all here, but this means, for example, that if I had three children born after January 1, 1977 and all three were boys, only one of them could be given a "boy's name" like Robert.

Of course, the legislation would contain a complete list of sexually-specific and sexually-indifferent names, and would be updated from year to year by an appropriate office in the Department of Health, Education and Welfare so that the public could be kept fully informed. Parents of newborn children would be required to file compliance reports, along with "Affirmative Action Plans" giving the family's goals in terms of names of future children. These goals must not be construed as quotas, however.

We do not anticipate an undue amount of litigation concerning the implementation of the guidelines to be administered by the Subcommission on Sexually Randon Naming of the Antidiscrimination Office (SSRNAO), but for the protection of the public there will be a Naming Appeals Board (NAB). The Subcommission will develop its policies with the cooperation of a panel of social workers, teachers, school administrators, psychologists, psychiatrists, psychiatric social workers, teachers' aides, oral surgeons, criminal lawyers and so on, and its budget for the first year should not exceed $218,000,000.

Compared with most other Federal legislation it will be a bargain.

Approved Publishers

ON MARCH 1, 1977, Radio Moscow broadcast the following item as part of its regular 6 p.m. (New York time) news broadcast, directed (in English) to American listeners:

"The newspaper Sovietski Kultura, published in Moscow, says the United States is opposed to equitable cultural exchanges. The Soviet Union has published over 6,000 translations of works by American authors reflecting a variety of historical periods, titles and philosophies.

"Only 500 titles, mainly Russian classics, have been published in the United States.

"American publications give preference to the past, while contemporary Soviet life is largely presented through the eyes of the so-called 'dissidents,' who depict a distorted picture.

"Theatres in Moscow, Leningrad and other cities have put on 35 productions by modern American authors. The number of plays translated from the Russian and staged in the United States is insignificant."

This quotation shows that when it comes to international understanding, nothing is more enlightening than the direct voice of the folks one is trying to understand. It would do us all good if more Americans listened to Radio Moscow once in a while, just as it would do the Russians good if more broadcasts from Western Europe could get through the short-wave jamming stations of the East.

What are the reporters and the paper Sovietski Kultura saying here? They are not lying, and they do not seem to be insincere in their expression of distress at the inequality of the "cultural exchange" between the U.S.A. and the Soviet Union.

It may be that by implication they are attempting to impugn the sincerity of American expressions of interest in detente, cultutal exchange and the like, but it is not necessary to imagine any such thing to realize what an awful confession of totalitarian thinking this news item amounts to--and it is all the more awful if it is wholly sincere.

To understand why, it is only necessary to imagine a similar pronouncement from the French national radio. Can one even imagine it? Read it again; it becomes laughable.

Does "France" translate 6,000 (or 60,000, or 600) works by American authors? Certainly not. Any Frenchman, or American, or Pole for that matter, can translate an American book into French and peddle the result in Paris and Marseilles. He needs permission of course from the author who owns the book, and probably must get a license or pay a tax in France, to be in the publishing business, and he must pay the American author and his translator the appropriate royalties and so on, but all this is no different from what he must do to publish a French book. It is done all the time, and it is of course a bit simpler if the book in question is old enough to be in the public domain.

And American publishing houses print French books here, in English, to the degree there is a market for them. They'll advertise too, to help create that market, if they think the public will catch on in the long run. And if they make a bad choice and lose on the investment, they'll be a bit more cautious the next time.

At the end of ten years, then, does the French Cultural Commissar tote up the number of American books sold in France and compare them with the number of French authors known in America? Does he find a score of 6,000 against 500, and broadcast a complaint that America "is opposed to equitable cultural exchanges?" Not so that anyone would notice it.

In France and America, books are written by people, printed by people, sold by people and read by people--not governments. There are no approved lists and there are hundreds of publishers, all free to do as they please. If something doesn't get printed, it is because nobody wants it, not because Little, Brown is against detente with France. If very few Iranian poets get translated into English, that is a natural consequence of the combined pressures of costs and public tastes, and is nothing to celebrate and nothing to regret.

The author of that piece in Sovietski Kultura does not understand the simplicity of this view, because it is a view natural only to one who has spent his life in freedom. To the Soviet writer there is no such thing as paying a royalty, publishing a book and selling it to people free to buy.

Certain duly approved authors, members of the Writers Union, get their books approved by government committees which are the only agencies of publication. What is printed, its quantity and its quality, is as determined by governmental policy as the size of armed forces and the number of pairs of size 11 men's shoes to be built in 1977.

Everything works that way, except for some shady backstreet maneuvering that has to be put down from time to time. (Fortunately there are mental hospitals for such people.)

How then should the Soviet writer realize, or even believe--if told--that the United States and France do things differently? To him this tale of the freedom of publication--and of shoe manufacture, for that matter--are capitalist propaganda. Rockefeller and IBM are well-known to control all the quotas, provided they don't antagonize the CIA.

If the U.S.A. doesn't print as many Russian works as the Russians print of ours, the explanation is obvious: the Soviet authorities are trying to do an honest job, a fair job, or presenting American culture to the Soviet people, while the American authorities are not reciprocating. Something must be done about this. Treaties are needed. The enemies of detente must be exposed. Our two great nations must move forward together in that spirit of friendship and blah, blah, blah.

The pity is that the fellow believes it!

Selling Russian Jews

SO THE Russians are selling their Jews again; what else is new? A higher price, a different customer? As if it made a difference. First, I'll review 1978; later on, 1915. Let the reader judge.

June 11, 1978: The New York Times, the headline: "Soviets Letting More Jews Go: U.S. Group Backing Trade Credits."

The first part is familiar. Jews by the thousands have been leaving the workers' paradise for civilized territory--if they can.

There are also "refuseniks" whose emigration request is denied, and who live in endless jobless limbo if not in jail. Those applicants who succeed do so after delay, harassment, anonymous phone calls, vandalism. They may wait years.

Why did the Soviets allow the emigration rate to rise this year? As the Times headline indicates, "credits" are the answer. The Trade Act of 1974 was passed by Congress precisely to induce a more liberal human rights posture in the Soviet Union; it deprived Russia of certain trade privileges worth many solid bourgeois rubles. The American Jewish Congress, one of several Jewish organizations, now believes, according to The Times article, that easing the ban on credits to Moscow might encourage an increase in emigration.

Other Jewish organizations, and most of the U.S. Congress disagree. The majority view seems to be that the Russian response has been grudging and too slight as yet, that the canny Marxists are still trying to sell their Jews at too high a price per Jew. When they come down a little, maybe we'll buy.

1915: World War I. "After nine months of bloody and difficult warfare, the Germans mounted a major offensive on the Russian front. By July they had conquered all of Russian Poland and were entering the Baltic and Western Russian provinces. The . . . Russian. . . rout. . . was largely due to a lack of munitions. . ."

The quotation is taken from my former colleague Michael Cherniavsky's fascinating book "Prologue to Revolution" (Prentice-Hall, 1967), most of which is his translation of the verbatim minutes of the secret meetings of the Government, the Council of Ministers of

Imperial Russia, as they met every few days during that terrible summer.

On July 16, Minister of War A. A. Polivanov declared, "I consider it my official and civic duty to declare. . .that the fatherland is in danger." He couldn't have been more right.

Money, for example. The last, billion ruble, bond drive had sold only half, and the money markets of the world were now closed, quite wisely, to Russian Imperial bonds. But Finance Minister Petr L'vovich Bark had an idea, which he argued on August 4 and 6:

If the council arranged some concessions to the Jews of Russia, he believed, it would be possible to induce certain foreign Jewish bankers, such as the Rothschilds of France, to swing a Russian loan, even at a financial loss. What "concessions"?

Well, up to 1915 Jews were not permitted to live in most of holy Russia. They could only live in Russian Poland and in the official "zone of settlement" in the west. But now the German advance was pushing thousands of Jews (and other refugees) eastward, even into the forbidden territories. The front was collapsing and the flood of refugees was irresistible.

Finance Minister Bark was not going so far as to suggest that Jews be granted all the rights of citizenship, or that they be permitted to own land, or to enter occupations and professions closed to Jews, or (God forbid!) to live in the holy Capital Cities of Moscow, Petrograd or Kiev.

No, only this: that as long as they were fleeing eastward anyhow, with the Army unable to keep them in the part of country they belonged in, well, maybe one could publish a decree granting them the right to enter those parts of Russia they were in, or nearly into. Then Rothschild in France would respond to this gesture of goodwill to his people by coughing up the billion rubles.

The debate makes entertaining reading: one wonders if the present Politburo uses similar language in debating today's Jewish question.

I. L. Goromykin, the chairman, said, "One must admit that concessions are inevitable . . . (but) . . . it is our duty to protect the rural districts from the Jewish invasion."

S. V. Rukhlov, Minister of Communications, was even more anxious that the Russian peasantry be protected from the "putrefying influence of Jewish neighbors.

Other ministers sought to reassure these idealists, pointing out that in reality the Jews were urban folk and would avoid the villages anyhow.

After some discussion of just which districts should figure in the decree, Minister of Agriculture A. V. Krivoshein cut to the heart of the matter, saying, "This is a detail . . . it is not worthwhile to clutter up with details an act that is designed to impress . . . One can always add the explanations later."

Not everyone favored such generosity. S. V. Rukhlov said, "All Russia is suffering from the war, but the Jews are the first ones to receive relief. My feelings, somehow, cannot accept this." Rukhlov refused to sign.

But Rukhlov lost. The decree was passed, a certain number of Jews were permitted by law to live in some of the Russian towns to which they had fled from the bombing and gunfire, and the Russian Imperial Government, all smiles, sent word to the Rothschilds to pay up.

1915! Today that terrible anti-Semitic Czarist regime has been replaced by a Marxist wave of the future, in which the exploitation of man by man is strictly forbidden. Still, there are always a few rubles to be earned by granting "concessions" to captive Russian Jews. Even in 1978.

Cultural Exchange

THERE IS no more certain proof of tyranny than the phenomenon of "cultural exhange"; and yet it seems that such exchanges always generate praise rather than scorn.

We all know how it goes: A bunch of Soviet and American diplomats and cultural attachés, well-paid and mightily photographed by the attendant press, put their pens to a solemn document permitting an American basketball team and symphony orchestra to tour the Soviet Union while a Soviet ballet troupe and circus tour the U.S.A. Corresponding exhanges of physicists, linguists, and certified safe social scientists complete the package.

Then to the microphones, where carefully-spoken spokesmen assure the world that we are seeing a historic milestone in the improvement of friendly relations between our two great peoples, a victory for detente, a defeat for the naysayers and warmongers--it can go on for half an hour without one unfamiliar word. Nasdrovie! Cheers! These fellows aren't well-paid for nothing.

Apart from the boredom, is there anything really wrong with all this? Should we not have cultural exchanges? Well, here's another way of looking at it.

In 1961, I was due for a leave of absence from the University of Rochester. My researches were going well, and I decided it was time to take advantage of the U of R custom of giving professors a year off with half-pay every seven years or so--provided the dean has reason to value that professor's services, and to believe the year will enhance his future value to the university.

I wrote to John Williamson, a mathematician in my line of work in Cambridge, England, asking if his department could provide me with office space for the year, access to the library and so on. I did what was necessary to rent a house in Cambridge for the year, and to rent out my own Rochester house for the same period. Everything worked out fine, and so I spent the academic year 1961-1962 happily and productively in Cambridge. My wife and two children too.

It is interesting to note that the house I had in Cambridge belonged to an economist named Robin Matthews who was spending his year at the University of California at Berkeley, having made much the same arrangements from his end as I had made from mine.

No government got in the way of either of us. We had passports, to be sure, as all travelers do, but there was no exchange, no signed treaty, no guff about improving relations between our two great nations. Matthews and I were simply free men in free countries, traveling where and when we liked, paying our way by one device or another, according to what we were able to swing.

Notice also that my arrangements were not the result of privilege or special luck. I had known the mathematician Williamson, by reputation of course, but I had never heard of Matthews at all--I got his house by advertising my need and then paying his price, and I got the invitation to Cambridge University by asking, as a known member of an international community of scholars.

No license required, no certificate, no medallion, no quota.

Compare our exchange with "cultural exchange." Could I have gone to Moscow on similar terms? Not on your life. There aren't any "houses for rent" columns in Pravda, and a visa for a year means a security check next to which our FBI looks like Little Orphan Annie. Besides, who would I be exchanged for? A ballet dancer? These things need negotiation. Signatures.

And in the other direction it gets even sillier. You can count the number of Soviet mathematicians visiting American universities for a year on one clumsy machinist's remaining fingers.

No, a "cultural exchange" is an occasion for sorrow, not celebration. We don't have cultural exchanges between New York and Oregon, between the U.S.A. and Italy; we just go. Some day, God willing, the whole world may be like that.

Meanwhile, a little honesty, please. The next time an American official signs a cultural exchange agreement, I would like to hear him say, not how pleased and proud he is at the blah blah blah, but rather, how much he regrets that the modern world should be reduced to this, that the document before him is the best his generation can do.

Then let us hear from the Soviet signer.

Helsinki Mathematical Congress

THE 1978 International Congress of Mathematicians opened in Finlandia Hall, Helsinki, at 9:30 a.m. of August 15. It is a beautiful concert hall, recently built, and was also the site of the 1975 conference which gave us the Helsinki Pact guaranteeing the security of the new borders in Europe and the rights of all human beings. The irony of this fact will soon appear.

We heard the Helsinki symphony orchestra play excerpts from Sibelius' music for Shakespeare's *The Tempest,* we heard opening addresses by the Lord Mayor of Helsinki, the Minister of Education of Finland and other such notable persons, and finally we saw the awarding of the four Fields Medals, which are our (mathematicians') equivalent of the Nobel Prizes. Four such medals are given at each Congress, and the Congress meets only once in four years.

The 1978 winners were Daniel Quillen and Charles Fefferman of the U.S.A., Pierre Deligne of Belgium, and G. A. Margulis of the Soviet Union. Rolf Nevanlinna, grand old man of Finnish mathematics and Honorary President of the Congress, presented the medals. Four winners were announced but only three were on the stage. Margulis, the Russian Jew, had been denied a visa to attend the Congress.

That Soviet mathematicians are often refused permission to attend international gatherings is well known. At Stockholm in 1962 and at Vancouver in 1974--Congresses I myself attended--I noticed that the program contained very many Soviet invited addresses, but that many of them did not in fact take place. At last week's Helsinki meeting there were 137 invited speakers, of whom all but 17 appeared and gave their lectures. Of those 17, 15 were Soviet. The missing speakers were not all Jews, of course, but among them were I. Bernstein, V. G. Drinfeld, D. Fuks, Ya. G. Sinai, and A. D. Wentzell.

Yet 1978 was special. Margulis was not merely an invited speaker, he was a Fields Medal winner. To the best of my knowledge this is the first time a Fields medalist has been prevented from appearing.

Following presentation of the prizes, we heard four lectures, one for each medal, explaining what the winner had done to earn his award.

Each lecture was delivered by an older master in the specialty of the winner under discussion (Fields medals are only given to persons less than 40 years old). The talk describing the researches of Margulis was given by Jacques Tits of France.

A Fields medal is not won by accident. Listening to Tits (and the three others too) made us all feel small in the presence of such work of genius, and yet proud that we live in a world where such fine things are accomplished. At the end, Professor Tits paused, looked up from his notes to the audience (three thousand of us gathered before him, fifty miles away from the Soviet Union), and spoke, as nearly as I can remember, as follows:

"This is not the place to indulge in polemic, but I cannot conclude this exposition of the recent work of Professor Margulis without expressing my regret that he is not able to be here today. I had hoped to meet him at the last Congress, in Vancouver in 1974, but as you all know he was not able to attend then either, though he had accepted an invitation to deliver an address to us at that time.

"Is it not a pity that I should know so well, but from publications only, the work of this young man of genius? This man whom I so much admire, and yet cannot have the opportunity to meet."

The audience applauded standing up, much as the signers of the Helsinki Pact of 1975 must have done when they had completed their noble draft concerning human rights. Noble sentiments in both cases, but while Jacques Tits spoke from the heart, his 1975 Soviet predecessors in that auditorium had spoken cynical lies.

Shall we go on with such cynicism?

Following the Congress I took a three-day tour to Leningrad, along with some other mathematicians. The facades of the fine old buildings along the river Neva are being refurbished in time for the Olympic Games. In the bookstores I saw special displays of books on sports, with the Olympic Games symbol of linked rings exhibited almost as prominently as photographs of Lenin and Breszhnev. Yes, The Soviets are already whooping it up.

Amateur athletics in the spirit of ancient Greece, with full television coverage! Russia will look grand on television, and Soviet 'amateur' athletes will clean up on the gold medals. Do we really have to lend ourselves to a year's worth of blatant lies, as we did at Helsinki in 1975? The Finns, who lost their richest forests to the Russian aggression of 1939, and who now live in the shadow of the bear, have no choice. They smile when the Russian commands. Must we too lend ourselves to this fraud of friendly sportsmanlike competition?

Why Study a Foreign Language?

I WAS impressed, when attending the International Congress of Mathematicians in Helsinki last August, at how universal has become the use of the English language among scholars of all nations. This was in considerable contrast to the situation at Stockholm meeting in 1962, which I also attended, where many of the talks were given in German, French or Russian.

I remember enjoying a brief work-out in German at that time. I met two East Berliners on a bus. My German isn't great, but it was enough so that I could astonish them with the information that Berthold Brecht and his works were well-known in America, even in Rochester, N.Y., home of the Eastman Kodak corporate imperialism.

In 1978, on the other hand, English was the language of virtually all the lectures, even when delivered by Germans, Romanians, Poles and Swiss, to whom in the old days French or German came more easily than English. Even the conversations in the hallways and bus tours were in English. If four mathematicians stood together, three of them German and the fourth Romanian, the conversation would go forward in English.

All this is a boon to Americans, who travel freely around the academic world using their own language, and a boon to the rest of the world as well, since one foreign language (English) learned well will provide as much convenience as in former times required a half-dozen. One might now ask, why should an American study any foreign language in school or college?

The University of Rochester requires every student in the College of Arts & Science to pass a foreign language proficiency examination. Whether the student learned that language in high school, at his mother's knee, at Berlitz or at the U of R doesn't matter so long as he shows a certain level of competence.

But if English is the common language of scholars the world over, why? There are several reasons.

For one thing, the man-in-the-street in France, Germany, Italy, Mexico--and Quebec--does not speak English. If one wishes to travel abroad, English may get him a meal at the Grand Hotel, but it will not allow much contact with the way life is actually lived in a foreign country.

But since there are so many foreign countries, all with different languages, this argument is not enough. I myself speak French and a little German, but I have found myself as helpless when visiting Greece, Russia and Portugal as if I had never studied any languages at all in school. However many languages one learns, most of the world will continue to be very foreign territory, linguistically speaking.

The best reason for knowing at least one foreign language is intellectual, not practical. One learns something about the nature of language itself, when one sees how a thought translates.

This one cannot understand via his own language alone. Languages are not codes for one another; if they were we could write our translations using a dictionary or a machine. But we can't. Each language organizes thoughts in a way peculiar to itself. To learn how the French or the Russians say something is to appreciate what part of your own thought is universal and what part is a mere curiosity of your own language.

The result is surprising, and uniquely educational. So much of what we believe is based on nothing but habit and the conventions of our own culture. Learning another language is one way among others, but a way that cannot be replaced by others, to discover that the obvious is not always true and that the truth is not always obvious. It is a way to discover in particular what we are really saying when we speak.

When a "short" sentence in English for example, turns out to require a cumbersome and lengthy translation in German, the reason is not that German is a clumsy language. The situation is just as often the other way around. What has happened is that an accident of English experience has made certain complex situations describable in a few English syllables. Turning it into German teaches us how complex the situation really was, something hidden from us by our familiarity with its brief English expression.

It is almost generally true that things are more complicated than they seem. Language often obscures as much as it reveals. Finding out how another culture--another language--deals with a familiar problem is one way to take the dust of familiarity off what could turn out to be a beautiful and complex idea. The lessons learned in this manner will far outlive our acquaintance with the language itself.

Even if we forget every word of French we may have learned in school, and never travel to Montreal, and never see a French film, and never read a French phrase in a chance novel, and never go into a French restaurant or read a label on a Bordeaux wine--even then, it will have been worthwhile once to have studied the language, and to have read a few chapters of something or other, for the experience of having once seen the world from another pair of eyes and ears, as if from within another's skin. That is the sort of experience that will not be forgotten with the word-lists.

Defending the Academy

THE ACADEMIC world is in constant need of defense--except sometimes. During the decade 1958-1968 we were, probably for the only time in history, universally approved.

Sputnik had made Education a national priority at just the time the population bulge was crowding the schools. The bourgeoisie anxiously hunted the "good college" that would accept its children; kids applied to a dozen to be sure of getting onto one.

The Atomic Energy Commission, National Science Foundation, Office of Naval Research, Ford Foundation, and a hundred others were getting in each others' way forcing money on deans and directors of research projects, however arcane. Aye, it was a heady time!

1968: The New Math and the Vietnam War fizzled at about the same time as a pot-smoking bunch of narcissists, calling themselves students, disrupted our colleges in the name of a new, higher morality. Their main success was to discredit the University as a haven for the intellect and its works. That the professoriate largely lay supine before this anti-intellectual onslaught, some of them celebrating the dedication and brilliance of the zealots, didn't help much. And then the job was completed by recession, inflation, and the decline in population growth.

Almost anyone can get into a "good college"--whatever that is--these days, and new Ph.D.'s hunt jobs as hopelessly as their ancestors of The Great Depression. It used to be said, in the 1932 Hoovervilles, that a Ph.D. and nickel would buy you a cup of coffee; well, the price has gone up.

This is not a joke that could have been made in 1960, and it shows that it is once again fashionable to malign the works of the mind. Well, maybe not fashionable, but at least decent. We academics are no longer sacred.

Sen. William Proxmire, for example, monthly announces his Golden Fleece Award, usually dedicated to some nonsensical-sounding research project. It is only a matter of time before the Absent-Minded Professor becomes once again the stock comedy figure he was in the days of Joe Penner and The Three Stooges.

Recent evidence for this prediction is found in a letter to the editor (D&C, Dec. 28) by Ray J. Guth, complaining that the Department of Energy is wasting millions of the taxpayers' dollars financing an experiment to determine whether or not all the matter in the universe "will decay to nothing in a time slot of about 10 billion billion billion years."

The substance of this complaint was answered by Prof. Harry Gove, chairman of the University of Rochester physics department (D&C letters, Jan. 5). I would add a few words of my own, even though I am no physicist, except that the defense of high-energy physics, or even the academic establishment, is not my purpose here. I mention the attack to illustrate the phenomenon.

Mr. Guth used the following phrases, "far-out theory," "way-out scientists," "asininity of these violations of sanity;" and he contrasted the "extravaganza" of the scientists with the needs of "our senior citizens and poor," (this phrase used twice, verbatim) and "concerned Americans."

Not a bad propaganda style; one has to look sharp to counter this sort of thing. Still, I do not complain of its existence. I'm glad we are no longer sacred. Indeed, I used to feel quite uncomfortable back in the days when to announce myself (in neutral company) a professor and mathematician would scare my interlocutor into gibbering or silence, according to his temperament.

Today, I hope it is better understood than it was in 1960 that a scientist is neither God nor Devil, but a certain sort of specialized professional, and that he, like anyone else, must justify his works if his neighbors are to provide him with food, clothing, and shelter. Therefore I believe it is no bad thing that Prof. Gove was made to defend the proton-decay experiment both for the public that reads it and for the sake of his own profession.

The philosopher John Stuart Mill, in his great essay "On Liberty," gave two main reasons for the toleration of dissent. One of them is a reason we would all think of immediately: it is that present 'truth' might in fact be wrong. Without permitting dissenting views to be heard, we would only cling to past errors, never learning anything new, and therefore never coming any closer to the real truth.

But a second, less obvious, reason is just as important. Suppose the current teaching *is* right. 2+2=4; no question about it. Even then, we must tolerate, even encourage, dissent, because it forces those of us who know the truth to reply, and in doing so to re-examine our reasons for thinking, or knowing, ourselves right. Without such debate our obvious truths become wordy formulas whose meaning we have forgotten.

In that golden decade of public approval, Universities grew lazy. Now that anti-intellectual attacks are bubbling up again, we academics have a chance to benefit from the necessary exercise of self-defense. To Prof. Gove I say, Give 'em hell, Harry! To his opposition I say, God bless the ignorant, for without you to teach we ourselves could not learn.

A Wineglass In The Teeth

MUSIC IS wonderful; I like music. I subscribe to the Philharmonic and any number of chamber concerts, and my house is full of moderately high fidelity electronics. Music is terrific.

Conversation too is great, one of the pleasures of life. Especially at the University, what a joy it is to lunch with experts--Persian history, plasma physics, Plato. I never leave the Faculty Club without having learned something new. 'Psychic income' is what the economists call this benefit, which is said to help make up for the increasing penury of our profession.

Well, no quarrel with that. And professors aren't the only people whose conversation I enjoy. Waiters, relatives, businessmen, children--there is a whole world out there and too short a life. Conversation, the exchange of thought, is one way to touch it all.

And, as everyone knows, wine helps. *In vino veritas:* man, do I like wine! In fact, I make wine myself, mostly from Delaware grapes grown down near Naples (N.Y.), but also some from California and some from vines I share with a friend in his Pittsford garden.

Once in a while I drink a truly great wine from France or Italy, but more often mediocre--and even downright miserable--just for the joy of trying out this or that, and to save money. Yes indeed, wine is wonderful.

Now, has anyone come up to me recently and shoved a glass of wine in my face, saying "Hey, Raimi, drink this!"--forcing it down my throat? Actually, no, but if it did happen I expect I'd offer a bit of resistance, to put it mildly. My benefactor might then say, "But wassa matter? Don't you like wine? This here is Chateau Lapuyiere-Frontenac Gafon 1970, man; I thought you *liked* wine!"

If he shoves that glass at me one more time, I'm thinking, I'll shove his teeth down his throat.

Luckily there aren't many people like that, maybe none. (If there were, you can be sure that the *quality* of the wine would not be the issue dividing us.) But when it comes to conversation, the world has lots of them: they are called bores.

Much as we may enjoy conversation, it is no pleasure when it is forced on us. A bore comes at you yammering no matter what you're in the middle of, playing the flute, watching Monte Python, reading. It doesn't matter what he's saying; it could even be something of great interest: plasma physics, Persian history, Plato. The point is that if this comes at a time when I'm not available for conversation, it is a bore, a nuisance, and a pain.

Though bores abound, we do have some defense. We can lock the door, or walk away, or tell them more or less politely to shut up. These tactics actually work, once you have a little experience.

Music, on the other hand, unwanted music, is an assault these days that only a dedicated hermit in the Gobi desert can avoid. The Mojave isn't good enough. Go into a bookstore, an elevator, a restaurant, a dentist's office, an airport; there it is, whether you asked for it or not. Walking the street, you pass pedestrians with gigantic portable radios on their shoulders, blaring. Go down to the secretary's office to check on a back-order and there it is, a tiny radio on the corner of the desk to confuse you.

Painters scraping the trim of your house? Music! Sunshine on the U of R fraternity quadrangle? Music from the biggest blasted speakers east of the Genesee! Call the auto dealer repair shop and get put on 'hold'? Mantovani! Wait in line at the bank while the guy in front pulls an endless sequence of papers out of an infinite supply of pockets? Music, music, music.

"Wassa matter, you don't like music?" Don't think I haven't been asked that, when I've mentioned my annoyance. The disease is in fact spreading, most recently to news broadcasts on radio and TV. Even in the prestigious and intellectual National Public Radio, the main points come at you from the interior of a quiet, ghastly, electronic pops band. The man talks, but who can understand? Background music, they call it; soothing.

It is no such thing. It is a bore, a wineglass in the teeth.

Is there any way to avoid it? Can one live without banks, groceries, airports, elevators? Maybe not. But hear this: If the invasion of the radio and television newscasts by music goes any further, I plan to start reading the newspapers again.

Chapter VI: **A Learned Controversy**

Wherein a newspaper column entitled *Decline of the English Language Isn't 'Nyoos'* elicits three letters-to-the-Editor and two personal replies.

A Learned Controversy

SOMEWHERE IN *Le Vicomte de Bragelonne,* I think, or *The Three Musketeers,* D'Artagnan found it necessary to enlist the aid of his friend Porthos on an adventure requiring travel to England. Porthos, a simple soul, suggested that their lack of knowledge of English might prove a hindrance; but D'Artagnan explained that there need be no fear, because English is, after all, "nothing but French badly pronounced."

Dumas did not footnote his novels, but even if he had been in the habit of pointing out to the reader that this or that episode in his romances was fictitious, or speculative--or true--I do not believe he would have included a footnote on the true relation between the French and English languages. That would have been to insult the audience, he would have thought, even the casual newspaper readers for whom he turned out his serialized novels.

My own experience now causes me to wonder. It may be that an irony or witticism such as D'Artagnan's will be generally understood, but that nevertheless *every* irony will find *someone* to misunderstand it. I present below one last newspaper piece of my own, with the headline given it by the Rochester Democrat and Chronicle editors as a title ("Decline of the English language isn't 'nyoo'"), followed by two letters-to-the-editor that appeared in the Democrat and Chronicle *letters* column in the following weeks. Then after some commentary of my own I print the two personal letters I wrote to the authors of the public letters. I end with a final letter-to-the-editor that was printed after I had exhausted my replies. I was by that time too disheartened to react.

****

Decline of the English language isn't 'nyoo'

by

Ralph A. Raimi

(as printed in the Rochester Democrat and Chronicle, January 4, 1978)

THE NEWSPAPERS have for many years been printing articles concerning the miserable state of the current use of the English language. Our language has of course been in a steady decline ever since it was called Latin, but the precise symptoms of that decline vary with the times.

I have my own complaint, but before presenting that latest wrinkle on an ancient face, let me review a few of the more popular lamentations of recent years.

Around 1936, when I was still a child, a professor of English at the University of Michigan wrote an article about the "howlers," as he called them, which had appeared in compositions by the students in his classes. The one I remember best, probably due to its prurient interest, concerned the reason for the founding of the American Colonies: "America was found as a haven for free lovers."

This example serves to show us that a howler of one generation becomes a simple truth to another. The professor thought there was a difference between "freedom lover" and "free lover"; today we know better.

Legal jargon, in the old days, was a more usual target. You know the sort of thing:

"In the event that the party of the first part fails, denies, refuses, avoids, demurs, snarls or otherwise noncomplies with the provisions of Section III A (c) (paragraph 2d) of this Contract, except as allowed under Title I (B) (a) (paragraph 3a, sub 2), petition for which must be made in writing within 30 days of receipt of Notice of Noncompliance, or within 60 days of . . ."

This isn't funny anymore. It is daily life for every taxpayer, businessman, driver, educator and Unemployment Insurance recipient. Satires on the government bureaucracy bring a hollow laugh at best, and at worst a hollow feeling in the thorax and purse.

Is there anything less fixed in amber, that we can laugh at in the secret hope that it will, like so much else under the sun, ultimately decay and die?

Well, yes, there is always the feminist jargon. A couple of years ago "spokesperson" and "chairperson" were worth a couple of laughs. Some wits among us thought to deride the trend by pointing out that consistency would dictate "huperson being" and maybe even "Federal Republic of Gerpersony." Alas, the spokespeople seem to have turned into a majority, and the chairpeople are firmly seated. No hope here.

Where else can some fragment of our language be saved? Human potential! Esalen and the "me" generation. Don't they ever have their jargon, or as they themselves would say, "Oh wow!" "Really, he's a very beautiful person. A real human being in his own right, you know. I can relate to him, y'dig? Empathize, like."

A little of this goes a long way, even in a lamentation. Maybe it will die, maybe not. One runs from it in horror, away from all these empathizing human beings--nobody seems to "sympathize" any more--towards what must finally be sanity: the business world.

No soft-headed encounter sessions here, no groovin' on the ineffable. Just straight talk that means something. English at its definite clearest, as used in the corridors of power, the board rooms of the multinational corporations, The Pentagon.

"Well, here's the nitty-gritty. If you want to be where it's at, in the forefront of the cutting edge of this thing, you'd better arrange your priorities, develop your game-plan, and make sure you offer a viable option. Bring along your laundry-list, watch out for a Catch-22, and keep your eye on the bottom line. Remember--no policy is carved on stone tablets in letters of gold."

This may be an improvement on the "in-depth relationships" and "ongoing situations" of the human potential types, but at this point in time I'd say it's lost its sheen.

And we're not done, we're not done. As long as there are sycophants in boardrooms and psychologists in the public schools, and that means as long as the sun keeps rising each morning, the jargon of their trades will live.

Is there anything at all, linguistically speaking, worth trying to put down?

Yes. One small thing. Very local. Very minor. Here, I think, sanity has a chance.

In the last year or two there has been a trend, on the local radio and television, towards the pronunciation of "afternoon" as if it were spelled "afternyoon." The word "too" is pronounced "tyoo," too. Let's stop that.

One can imagine the history of this disease. Consider the two words "few" and "new." The first is pronounced "fyoo," of course. But the second, while pronounced "nyoo" in England, has been as frequently pronounced "noo" in America.

Someone has obviously decided that it is lower-class or ignorant to do this, and that "nyoo" for "new" is classier. So far, so good: who can quarrel? Both pronunciations are familiar, and both have historical roots.

But to become so obsessed with gentility, or Anglophilia, as to transfer that y sound to every word with an "oo" syllable is mindless and ridiculous. And yet it is gaining. "Afternyoon" and "tyoo" are already common; soon brides will be saying "I dyoo," and retired radio announcers will spend their declining years puttering about in the "gyarden."

Enough! Other novelties in our language may have had some purpose, if only evil, and so have had some reason to attract a following. This particular complication, however, is totally senseless. It merits obloquy at least, and scrupulous excision.

****

(Rochester Democrat and Chronicle, January 21, 1978)

Is Raimi's article a put-on?

ACCORDING to our colleague, Prof. Ralph Raimi, "our language has . . . been in a steady decline ever since it was called Latin . . ." (D&C Opinion 2, Jan. 4).

Whatever qualifications Prof. Raimi may have as a mathematician, we take strong exception, not only to the sense, but also to the "facts" he presents.

Unless Prof. Raimi's meaning has somwhow been lost in the process of editing, it is as though everything known about the nature of language and of

historical linguistic change had been completely ignored.

To view change as "decline" is utterly false. The citations of "yoo" pronunciations for "oo" are classic instances of hypercorrections—themselves well-known attestations of sound change.

English, a Germanic language, has never been called "Latin" until this week. One is tempted to wonder whether Prof. Raimi's piece is not a put-on.

CHARLES M. CARLTON, DENNIS FRENGLE, FREDERICK W. LOCKE, ANTANAS KLIMAS and R. V. HARRINGTON, Department of Foreign Languages, Literatures and Linguistics, The University of Rochester

****

(Rochester Democrat and Chronicle, January 21, 1978)

English has never been called 'Latin'

SHAME ON Prof. Ralph A. Raimi (D&C Opinion 2, Jan. 4) for stating in his article that English has been in "decline ever since it was called Latin."

English never has been called Latin. It is placed in the Indo-European language group under the sub-family Germanic.

Latin is in the same language group but under the sub-family Italic.

A Celtic language was being spoken in Britain when the Romans arrived in 55 B.C.

Over some 400 years of Roman occupation many Latin words were absorbed, as were many words from the Vikings, Danes and Saxons who invaded the islands after Rome's departure.

By 1066 A.D. the "English" language again absorbed some Latin words—indirectly—with the arrival of William the Conqueror and his Norman followers.

One of the great things about English is its ability to absorb and adopt new expressions and to change with the times.

English has continued over the centuries to borrow from foreign languages so that now most languages of the world are represented to some extent' making English a rich and flexible means of communication for millions of people.

Today we use words of Latin background along with words of non-Latin background. For example: to "get gifts" (non-Latin) or to "receive presents" (Latin) are equally acceptable phrases.

I do agree wholeheartedly with Prof. Raimi in that there is today a lack of good English in use.

I am particularly appalled at the quality of English spoken by commentators on ABC, CBS and NBC news—people who should know better.

Also, it is rather frightening to listen to some of our federal, state and local legislators and hear the poor quality of English used.

VALERIE T. FREUND, 155 Yarkerdale Dr.

****

The letter of Valerie T. Freund was earlier sent to me personally, under a covering letter (which I do not reproduce here) explaining that she had sent the newspaper the other letter. Her personal letter repeated some of the arguments against English's having been called Latin, and spoke of her home town, London, and the probability that *Londinium* is a Latinized Celtic phrase. I mention all this because my answer to Mrs. Freund, printed below, refers to two letters and to the word *London.* The misunderstanding of my intention by Ms. Freund did not particularly surprise me, or irritate me, and so my answer to her was a straightforward explanation.

The letter of the five linguistics professors was another matter. Not only are they better educated than the generality of readers, and not only should they be an example to the community in their ability to read and interpret the written word, since they are professors of language, but three of the five had known me personally for years and should have known what sort of person I am and what my degree of understanding is, of history, linguistics and so on.

Professor Harrington, for example, was for some years Chairman of the Department of Foreign Languages, Literatures, and Linguistics (called FLLL) while I was Associate Dean for Graduate Studies. This meant that I governed the budget for graduate fellowships and teaching assistantships in his department, and that I was Chairman of the faculty committee that monitored the academic quality of his graduate programs. I often conferred with Harrington, tête-à-tête or in committee, on the courses he offered, the quality of his graduate students and the size of their stipends, the appointment of new professors, and the language requirements for undergraduate students. I had written him dozens of letters, chatted with him when I met him on campus, and even participated as an 'outside examiner' on a couple of Ph.D. final examinations of FLLL students.

In all this time Harrington treated me like an educated adult and not a child or idiot. Never once did he betray anything but the greatest respect for my understanding of language and linguistics (though of course I was no specialist). If someone had suggested to me in 1972 that Harrington believed me ignorant of the Germanic roots of modern English--something I first learned about in the eighth grade, in fact--I would have been incredulous. Is this the way Chairmen always look on Deans?

So it will not do to say these men did not read the article I wrote, for even if they had read only the phrase they quoted they should have known I was not capable of believing it literally and publishing it authoritatively as truth. If the quoted phrase (which had been repeated in the newspaper display as a large-type boldface subheading, by the way) had been all they read, they were guilty of leaping to conclusions by ignoring the context, but I suspect that at least some of them must have read the whole article, even if lightly. They are scholars, after all.

What should a literary scholar have noticed here? In the rest of this volume I do not comment on the excellence of my own prose, rather leaving it to the reader to discover; but in the present case I must analyze my intentions, as expressed in prose, in some detail. Consider the first three sentences:

1. The newspapers have for many years been printing articles

concerning the miserable state of the current use of the English language.

2. Our language has of course been in a steady decline ever since it was called Latin, but the precise symptoms of that decline vary with the times.

3. I have my own complaint, but before presenting that latest wrinkle on an ancient face, let me review a few of the more popular lamentations of recent years.

I believe that anyone who reads all three of these sentences, whether or not he has met me and argued academic policy with me, and whether or not he goes on to read any part of the rest of what I wrote, has here enough clues to choke a horse.

Sentence #1 is a simple declarative sentence and a true one. The newspapers *have* been printing such articles. Notice, though, what the articles I refer to are about: not the miserable state of *English,* but the miserable state of its *use.* I do not believe the language is in trouble, and indeed my own complaint, presented at the end of the article, concerned a rather minor matter of pronunciation; therefore I was careful to say precisely what I meant in my opening sentence.

Sentence #2 turns ironic. I wanted the reader to understand that I was not to be identified with the schoolmarmish approach to language orthodoxy. If people want to say "It's me", I am not the sort to deliver thunderous warnings about predicate nominatives. I wanted to convey lightly that I do not "view with alarm" every novelty or non-standard usage. Therefore I tried to get the reader to smile with me about the 'decline' of the language--a language that he and I both perfectly well know is serving our purposes. How?

I begin Sentence #2 with 'of course'. Now when one is offering a controversial proposition seriously, he doesn't say 'of course'. When one is putting forward an outrageous proposition for humorous effect, 'of course' (I hope) adds to the outrage, thereby making the status of the remark plainer.

For example, "One plus one equals eleven" is certainly a false statement, but I have heard it as a sort of joke (back in the third grade, I think). While this is a poor joke, I can easily imagine a situation where one could say,

"It has long been known, of course, that one plus one equals eleven. . . . ," and then go on to some less obvious fallacy this one was intended to illuminate by analogy.

So it was with my decline of English, but I went even further than "It has long been known, of course. . ." in surrounding the false statement with additional outrages. I said the language had been in decline "ever since it was called Latin." Now everybody knows (or it seemed to me when I wrote this that everybody knew) that English was never called Latin; it *couldn't* be. Even if one were unaware that Old English is more of an ancestor of English than Latin is, logic alone shows that 'Latin', a modern English word, could not serve as an ancient name. One cannot, after all, say "English used to be called 'Old English'" either. In some sense, English used to *be* Old English, but one would have to know Old English to know what Old English was called, for I am convinced the Saxons did not call Old English 'Old English'.

In other words, the whole form of the phrase "ever since it was called Latin [or whatever]" is ridiculous. There is *no* name that can be put in place of 'Latin' to render the sentence true. I had counted on this logical silliness to reassure the reader that I was not serious about the decline, at the same time that I was averring that it had been going on for several thousand years, this length of time being automatically implied by my naming of a language that old. And my indication of that long a time, whether by naming Latin or by any other device, was itself a sign that I was not serious about decline, for a 2000 year decline surely could not leave us with even the poor excuse for a language we now have.

Even this observation doesn't exhaust the sentence, which concludes, ". . . but the precise symptoms of that decline vary with the times."

Now a 'decline' is what people in the 19th Century used to call a disease of some sort, saying of someone, "He went into a decline, and died." What disease can it be, then, whose symptoms "vary with the times"? Any doctor will tell you that the most important such disease is hypochondria, i.e., there ain't no such illness.

What with the 'of course', then, and the outrageous suggestion that English was once called Latin, and the 2000 year history of decline, and the observation that the varying symptoms of that decline suggested hypochondria as the underlying disease, I felt fairly secure against misunderstanding. It was plain that I was mocking the pedantic approach to 'correct English'.

But just to make sure, I put in Sentence #3. I called the complaints of the decline of English "lamentations." Does anyone with a serious complaint call it a lamentation these days? And to talk about "the more *popular* lamentations of recent years" is surely to mock the idea even more. My own complaint is further downgraded by calling it the "latest wrinkle on an ancient face," a wrinkle being not very much in the way of disease, after all, and even less noticeable where wrinkles have been accumulating for millennia.

Well, I thought of explaining all this to my colleagues in FLLL, and even wrote part of it out, but finally changed my mind. They *are* literate after all, and so I wrote in the form printed below. I have reason now to believe they understood it. What Ms. Freund understood of my letter I never found out. But then, after all this, I picked up the Democrat and Chronicle on February 9 and read the letter of Judith Eakins Kiehl.

****

THE UNIVERSITY OF ROCHESTER
DEPARTMENT OF MATHEMATICS
MATHEMATICAL SCIENCES BUILDING
ROCHESTER, NEW YORK 14627

Phone 716-275-4411

January 16, 1978

Ms. Valerie L. Freund
155 Yarkerdale Drive
Rochester, New York 14615

Dear Miss Freund:

Thank you for your letter - two letters, in fact! I don't usually receive two letters at a time.

My comment "ever since it was called Latin" is a joke. It is several jokes, in fact, which is itself a joke, since a singular subject "It" gets thereby a plural predicate nominative "several jokes".

But to return to English and Latin: of course English was never called Latin. It wasn't called German or Anglo-Saxon, either, or Sanskrit, or even Middle English. English is; and what was (in the Middle Ages, say, or under Hadrian) was simply another language.

My point was this, that every language has ancestors, and that during everyone's lifetime a certain part of the ancestor language dies in favor of what soon will become the standard, both as to pronunciation and usage. Furthermore, that this constant change is invariably lamented by persons sensitive to the virtues of part of what is being lost, but that, since such changes have been taking place since Hadrian built his wall, and longer, a certain philosophical acceptance is called for.

To say English used to be called Latin is as sensible as to say John Smith used to be called Jones, in that his mother's father was named Jones. To be tedious, one would say John Smith's family used to be called Jones, or at any rate part of his family. But Grandpa Jones is not John Smith and never was; no more is or was English Latin or German.

On the other hand, there did exist a man sometime in the past two thousand years whose father taught him to say Londinium, but whose grandchildren were babbling on about London. That man surely believed his language was on the rocks. Whether that man called his language Latin, Saxon or English, I cannot say.

Sincerely yours,

Ralph A. Raimi
Professor of Mathematics

****

THE UNIVERSITY OF ROCHESTER

NTRAMURAL CORRESPONDENCE

January 24, 1978

Professors Carlton, Frengle, Harrington, Klimas, Locke
FLLL

Gentlemen:

I beg you to imagine that you had written an Op Ed article in the local newspaper, intending to make a point about the nature of scientific inference, especially with regard to the misuse of mathematical and statistical methods. You are not to imagine yourselves scornful, or opposed to the use of these sciences, for you know them to be honorable when rightly used. No, your purpose is to attack, in an urbane, possibly somewhat humorous, manner, those who through ignorance or malice, and often in the name of science itself, inhibit its progress and corrupt its application.

Imagine then, that after lamenting (in your article) certain low practises, solecisms and half-truths, or perhaps even at the outset of your article, you have occasion to refer to the old schoolboy witticism that one plus one makes eleven. It seems relevant to your argument that you do this, and the needs of your art cause you to put the matter in the following way:

"The reputation of mathematics has of course been in a decline ever since it was discovered that one plus one equals eleven..."

A weak joke, perhaps, but (I ask you to imagine) illustrative of something you have in mind. Perhaps the 'decline of mathematics' is to serve as a leitmotif in what follows, though you and your readers are naturally aware that mathematics has been respectable and increasingly valuable since Plato, and that one plus one has always been two.

Imagine further that in the following weeks there appeared a Letter to the Editor of that same newspaper, signed by five members of the University of Rochester Department of Mathematics, some of the text of which was as follows:

"Whatever qualifications Professors Carlton, Frengle, Harrington, Klimas, and Locke may have as linguists, we take strong exception, not only to the sense, but also to the "facts" they present. While it is true that the placing of two copies of the symbol denoting 'one' side by side produces the conventional representation of 'eleven', such a juxtaposition cannot be called addition.

"'Plus' is not the word to use here, since the mathematical 'plus' is a technical term meaning something quite different from the mere notion of accretion conveyed by the same word in common parlance. Thus the 'discovery' that one plus one equals eleven is erroneous. Indeed, it never took place, and to ascribe a (fictitious) decline in the reputation of mathematics to this non-event is to compound the error into a historical jumble that cannot go unchallenged.

"One is tempted to wonder whether Professors Carlton, Frengle, Harrington, Klimas, and Locke are not putting us on!"

I have abbreviated this imaginary reply to avoid tedium, but its tenor is clear enough. Having imagined that you have read it in the newspaper, what would you answer the learned professors of mathematics?

Would you take up your five pens and write once more, solemnly assuring the readers that you did not truly believe that one plus one was eleven? That what appeared to be a debate on the history of the reputation of mathematics was in fact only the result of a grievous misconception on the part of your mathematical colleagues, who had unaccountably misread your intention?

I think not. I believe, in fact, that you would soon come to the conclusion that silence were best, and that a public reply would benefit nobody. A public reply would, I am sure you would realize, only serve to demonstrate to the public that academics can read as badly as anyone else, and that even five mathematicians can mistake wit for error by ignoring the context of the phrase that erred.

Sincerely yours,

Ralph A. Raimi

Ralph A. Raimi
Professor of Mathematics

RAR:ml

****

(Rochester Democrat and Chronicle, February 9, 1978)

Languages change

CONCERNING the essay of Professor Ralph Raimi (D&C Opinion 2, Jan. 4): Not to worry, Professor Raimi.

Languages do not die, fade away, or even "decline." They just constantly change, making English words of what has been named something else another time, transforming today's "correct" phrase into next year's "error."

The fellow who says "I ain't done nothin'" is, linguistically, communicating as effectively as the more socially acceptable gentleman who "hasn't done anything." The only people who are (unduly) concerned with the natural processes of language are the purists, prescriptivists and snobs who do not understand the principles of linguistic change, and clutch desperately in their ignorance to what they believe are "the rules," professor.

Incidentally, Prof. Raimi's own writing style is so unclear as to leave a mystery whether he intended a parody of contemporary usage, a standard protest of "dying" tradition, or both. His next free-lance effort, we hope, will deal with the field of mathematics.

JUDITH EAKINS KIEHL, 48 Lanvale Park

Chapter VII: **Two Pessimistic Essays**

On Liberty

LIBERTY IS after all only a pleasure, like wine and sex. Some prize it highly, while others would trade it away voluntarily for food and security, or for some advantage to the moral structure about them.

Still, people who fight for liberty, who risk their lives and fortunes in pursuit of liberty, seem to be more highly honored in newspaper editorials and Commencement speeches than are those who take the same risks in the fight for women and wine. I believe the reason is not so much that there is seen to be a difference between all these pleasures, as that a fighter for liberty is generally seen to be struggling on behalf of more people than just himself, while strugglers after material things merely look greedy.

Social reformers like Lenin and Hitler were much honored by their partisans even though neither promised liberty. Lenin promised bread and Hitler promised glory, but both these commodities were to be widely available, they said. A large public therefore felt it had a stake in the outcome, even though in at least one case the principal result was to be material gain.

There is one notorious exception to the observation, that we honor those whose labors appear to promise something to a large number of us: love. All the world, it is said, loves a lover, smooths his path, sings of his success or his sorrow; and yet his quest is for a good of value to himself alone. And that most assuredly not liberty.

Is it that we take a voyeuristic pleasure in a lover's endeavors? I think not. At least Romantic Europe surely honored Lord Byron for more than this. There is one more ingredient not yet mentioned that must enter an activity truly honored by humanity or a large part thereof: religion.

To put it in 17th Century terms, we honor those who are plainly doing the Lord's work. Indeed, they even honor themselves. Knowing their selflessness in the service of the Lord, they develop a confidence impervious to criticism, prison or exile. We would call them arrogant if we weren't so busy praising them. Luther and Metternich, can they be told apart? Only in that one served the Lord and the other served the

Bourbons.

During the Romantic Movement, then, and it is not quite over, the lover was doing the Lord's work. A Japanese of the time would have been quite puzzled by the lover's popularity. Earlier, during the 17th Century in England, the pamphleteer and the Puritan fought for liberty so that God's work could be done without the corrupting influence of Popish governors. From that time, and the American struggle of the 18th Century, our own copy books have drawn the lesson that liberty is the value we honor most, but that is only half the lesson. Liberty *to serve the Lord* is what it was about.

With the decline of Puritanism in the present century in America and Western Europe, the ideal of liberty has been losing its place at the top of our list of desires. Security, economic well-being, ecological balance, peace; these are some of the things we look to our leaders to bring us, in most cases at the expense, each of them, of a part of the liberty our ancestors won under God's banner two and three hundred years ago.

What would we do with liberty if we had it, after all? Save having to pay union dues in a closed shop? Risk losing our tenured or guild-controlled employment? Leave our wives, shoot heroin, carry placards in front of the White House, desert the Army, travel to Albania, drive on the wrong side of the street, charge usury? In most cases we prefer the restrictive alternative, so long as we are sure the restriction lies upon our neighbor as upon ourselves.

There is no longer a Lord's work to be done with liberty; that Lord is dead. We may now balance the pleasures of liberty against the pleasures of wine, woman and song, or any other competitor for our praise and our effort, and strike the balance that suits us. Lip service to liberty will not soon die, but the true servants of liberty are generally called reactionaries when they are noticed at all.

The Lord's work of the 20th Century has very little to do with liberty, and if any lesson is to be drawn from History, it is that the Lord's work has always come first.

Vested Interests

ALL MY childhood was spent among Communists, in Detroit, Michigan, U.S.A. When I was six I went with my mother to spend a few days in a cabin on the outskirts of a place called *Workers Camp,* a summer camp for children. I was too young to be a full member, but my older brother saluted the red flag every morning and sang *The Internationale* while I watched from a distance, aching to be old enough to participate. The words as I heard them are still fresh in my mind:

Tis the final cornflake,
Let each stand in his place...

My understanding was dim. In my secular school of the winter season I similarly memorized the familiar

One nation invisible with liberty
And justice for all.

I could believe anything.

I believed in the wickedness of the Vested Interests, of course. My brother explained *surplus value* to me: The bosses pay the workers less than the value of their labor, stealing the difference with the aid of policemen and injunctions. That difference is called *Surplus Value.* Since the workers can't buy back their product, having been paid less than its value, the bosses have to find other markets for their goods. Thus *Imperialism,* serving the dual function of creating a market for surplus goods, and providing a cheap source of raw materials and labor.

Foreign workers, I was told, were notoriously underpaid. (So were Americans, who worked in sweatshops, but this was not part of the foreign trade discussion.) Therefore imports were cheap, undercutting American prices, especially of union-made goods. Tariffs and strikes were needed to prevent this.

It was not explained to me how the underpaid foreign workers could, via Imperialism, be forced to buy the surplus goods our own workers couldn't 'buy back'. There were other inconsistencies that troubled my rather mathematical mind, especially as my sixth year gave way to my seventh, eighth and ninth.

Reading The Daily Worker, which occupied much of the first years of my literacy, didn't help much. The same few elementary lessons, much as my brother had given them to me, were there repeated time and again, but with no greater depth than the first time around.

There were cartoons, too, as if humor, however uncongenial to the Communist spirit, must have its due. The recurrent themes and caricatures were pretty much drawn from *Krokodil,* I learned later, though they were supposed to have their roots in American experience as firmly as Skeezix and Dagwood Bumstead. The resulting wit was a bit strained.

Most easily remembered was a figure in frock coat and top hat, a vest with many buttons, crossed by a heavy watch chain hung in two comfortable catenaries. He was well-fed, this nameless gentleman, and looked like William Howard Taft except when his head was replaced with the drooling countenance of a wolf or other predator.

Usually pictured in the company of two bulging duffel bags marked $$$, he represented The Bosses without question, and the duffel bags obviously contained surplus value. Even the fact that he invariably wore a vest was not fortuitous, whatever sort of head his silk hat surmounted: he and his kind were the Vested Interests.

Schwab, Schwab, Charlie Schwab,
Life and Happiness you rob---
From the workers in the mills
To the miners in the hills.

The moral choice was not difficult; despite my troubled understanding I knew which side I was on. The man in the silk hat must no longer grind the faces of the poor, and the People must rule in his place. This can be done: In Soviet Union they are doing, no? So much for 1930.

****

Now many years have passed. Old Isaac Smullin, who founded *Worker's Camp,* lived (alas) to see the Molotov-Ribbentrop pact and worse. For my part, I learned that 'vesting' has more than sartorial significance.

I belong by virtue of my employment to a retirement plan which has the feature that all my contributions, and the contributions of my employer, are vested in myself. That is, whatever that annuity account it worth today, it belongs to me. I shall draw from it on an appropriate actuarial basis beginning at my retirement whether I keep my present job or quit it, or displease my employer and am fired, or displease my neighbors and go to jail. Though I should be hanged as a traitor, my heirs and assigns will receive its ('death benefit') value according to my direction.

Not every pension plan works this way, as has been made clear in recent Congressional hearings into the subject. Many a worker has contributed, often via union check-off, to a company or union-organized plan, and found that he lost all benefits if he quit his job before 15 years' service, or the company went out of business, or the union fund was badly managed or actuarially unsound. Often his payments were attractively low causing him to believe his plan had some special virtue, when the reason was that the plan's managers knew the pay-off would be to many fewer people than had contributed.

This kind of plan is the opposite of a vested interest; it makes the insured dependent on the good-will of his employer or his union, or it limits his mobility. The title is not in him, but in a collective of some sort, like old-age pensions in Russia. The thought of a retired Russian emigrating to Israel and subsisting on old-age pension checks from Moscow gives one to smile, but I can do the corresponding thing when my time comes, if I like.

The Soviet Union, it should be observed, operates in this way not merely with respect to retirement income or medical care, but with respect to absolutely everything: job, house, liberty itself. None of these is in the absolute possession of its holder. Let once the job-holder signal his desire to emigrate--not that this is the only sin against the State--and his job, his apartment, his mobility are gone. Even in normal circumstances his vacation--two weeks in the Crimea--may be a feature of his job; he takes a train with a group of fellow-workers. Much of what he has is 'on the house', privilege as easily revoked as given. What he 'owns' is a fiefdom; he is in thrall to the collective.

****

I would not wish to set up too sharp a distinction between the Russian collectivity and the American individual liberty. Each country has elements of the other's style, if not its formal system. Sinclair Lewis

(Main Street) and Ring Lardner *(Haircut)*, for example, have showed how illusory is even the American liberty in some respects. We may have legal title to bank account and automobile, but the good opinion of our neighbors may be necessary to any use of these benfits. This lesson is a recurrent theme in American literature; we have seen it in O'Hara's *Appointment in Samarra* and as recently as in the film *Easy Rider,* where the young men with offensive haircuts are simply murdered by representatives of an outraged community.

On the other hand, this theme is not recurrent in Soviet Russian literature--it doesn't appear at all. That alone should be proof that while American individual liberty has its troubles, Russian liberty of this kind hardly exists and is certainly not accorded to writers. We have enough independent knowledge of this, too, in the cases of Daniel, Sinyavsky, Pasternak and Solzhynitzn, not to have to belabor the point. But the fact that Solzhynitzn could exist at all, write and be printed at least abroad, shows that there is a chink in the armor of Russian collectivism corresponding to the slight imperfection of American liberty. No system is perfect.

The question is, which way are we headed? Will the struggle between the collective ideal and the ideal of individual liberty continue, or end in a victory or in a compromise? There is a popular theory which speaks of a "convergence" of the American and Soviet ways. Generally it is the two economic systems these theorists are thinking of, and they have some evidence for convergence in the relative growth of the public sector in the economies of the "capitalist" nations in recent years. The corresponding evidence of growth of the private sector in Russia is, however, missing, and the Russian attitude towards opening up the economic system in Hungary and Czechoslovakia (1956-1968) shows that the convergence, if it does take place, will not be to a point midway between our systems.

I believe the same direction will be the direction of our 'convergence' in the rest of the spectrum of human activity. To be brief, collectivism will win. I don't like the prospect and I shall fight against it, but I see very little hope.

Though it is a tired analogy I can think of nothing better than the decline and fall of the Roman Empire to illustrate our present position. I know perfectly well that in Europe in the year A.D. 400 (say) there was no clear-cut struggle between the forces of darkness and the forces of light. Rome was already half-Christian; France was half-Roman. The defenders of the old order supported an increasingly gloomy and pointless tyranny while the barbarians fought for liberty of a sort--certainly for self-determination.

Yet had I been there, on the Rhine or on the Po, I would have struck my blow for a few more years of literacy, music and paved highways, before the inevitable darkness came down upon Europe.

Darkness? To many a mind it was light. Within a century or two the word of Christ's sacrifice had penetrated every corner of Europe--and indeed, if one takes a largish view of Mohammed's teaching, to every corner of the Mediterranean as well, and as far as even Alexander had carried the teaching of Aristotle. Gone was that large domain of social anarchy that had disturbed, enlivened and enriched the ancient Mediterranean; in its place was the new Christian Europe, where all was fixed in duty, custom and the will of God.

So perfect was the spirit of community--at least where the theory of feudalism was well observed--that a man hardly owned the shirt on his back, much less land, gold or stores of wheat, except at the pleasure of his lord. The serf was tied to the property, the lord to the service of his Prince, and the Prince to the Church. No interest, no wealth, no expectation was vested in an individual. All was community: land used at the discretion of the community, prices set at the community level of fairness, wages (if any) the same. Whatever was not forbidden was compulsory, and above all was the obligation to believe in the truth of the Church and the religious necessity of the feudal order.

Most people were poor, of course, since technology was primitive and large numbers of servants of the Church and the military were not engaged in producing goods, but poverty was not as synonomous with despair as it became during the industrial revolution. The community cared for its aged and its ill, as much as was possible, and protected its members from the loneliness that must have been known in ancient cities as it is in modern cities too. The only cost was collectivism, an ideal best exemplified in the monastary system which grew up later in the age of faith. One gave up all title to property and thoughts of one's own, to win a world both here and hereafter.

That world was his own, the monk's very own world, in some sense, but the ownership was not vested in him as an individual. He could not resign and take his share away with him. If he changed his mind on some important point of politics or religion he could lose that share of collective ownership he enjoyed, and maybe his life.

So with the serf, the baron and the king. Kings too were known to walk barefoot in the Alpine snow for penance, or (in legend) to change places with their own court jesters, magically, and learn the meaning of abasement. "He hath struck down the mighty from their seats and exalted those of low degree," was the lesson taught Robert of Sicily.

There were exceptions; there are always exceptions. Like the rat who ("stout as Julius Ceasar") swam to the far side of Weser, avoiding the fate his fellows met dancing to the Pied Piper's tune, there survived some remnants of antique individualism through even the darkest years of Christendom. A handful of travelling clowns and troubadours, the shifting pockets of miscreant Jews, a few seamen, merchants, pirates, highwaymen--who could tell them apart?

Usuary was a crime as grave as murder, but some money was lent and borrowed just the same. A merchant who bought at one price and sold at a higher was in danger of at least his immortal soul, maybe an Auto da Fe, but he was never quite stamped out. The baker who in a famine year thought to get some wheat by paying more and raising his price for bread correspondingly--that baker might well have been destroyed by the righteous townfolk, cast in some Godly dungeon and his bakery burnt. Still, the bakery would open again, perhaps with new management but surely with the higher price list dictated by economic necessity.

There were exceptions, yes, but it was a hard choice: gold of one's own, but no protection of manor, monastary or village. Few could afford to choose the path of liberty.

Those few who did grew in numbers with each century, until with the great Reformation and splintering of the Christian Church, and with the crushing of the danger of Moslem invasion, the economic outlaws became a recognized necessity in society; guilds of merchants and manufacturers as valid in their way as manors and villages based on land. By the time of the Industrial Revolution it seemed that commerce had won the day. Even the laws of princes vested wealth in individuals. One could own his shirt, his house, his gold, his fleet of ships, and could set whatever price he wished on goods or services. Usury became interest, piracy became trade, and heresy became an ancient right of Englishmen.

Still--just as some ancient individualism lived in spirit through the dark and middle ages, incubating like winter wheat until the sun returned, so has some medieval collectivism always survived the revolutions of Copernicus and Adam Smith. Mercantilism, the earliest attitude of princes towards the necessities of trade, was itself not quite the liberty Adam Smith urged on the future. The very guilds and unions which threaded the hope of liberty through the secular needle's-eye gradually turned into brakes on the progress of capitalism: Luddites destroyed machines just as food rioters had levelled bakeries six hundred years before.

Philosophers and seers have never been wanting to extoll the virtues of the collective over the entrepreneurial. What high school student has not read Oliver Goldsmith's *The Deserted Village:*

> *Ill fares the land, to hastening ills a prey,*
> *Where wealth accumulates and men decay.*

This was written in the 18th century in stalwart opposition to the very revolution in agriculture (and all other forms of productive enterprise) which was to end by banishing hunger in Britain. The poem celebrated the medieval ideal of commonality, an ideal that had never died.

Finally, just when the development of free commerce was marking its greatest triumphs, the collective ideal was finding in Karl Marx its mightiest voice since Jesus.

The symmetry is not as complete as this; if it were, human history would truly be as cyclic as Spengler imagined, successive waves of collectivism and individualism, the seed of each surviving the fruiting of the other. In fact history does not repeat itself wholly, or at any rate does not seem to have done so yet. I doubt that the typical merchant of ancient Rome was as free of his Prince as a merchant of 17th Century Holland, or any ancient artist as sure of his bank account as Franz Hals. The modern vesting of wealth and consequent freedom of choice in an individual--in every individual who wished it--was almost a new development in social history.

It may be, in the same way, that the loss of these rights is and will be more complete in the collectives of the 20th and 21st centuries than it ever was in the feudal manor, or even under the Benedectine Rule. The medieval Jew could still carry his Torah to Germany when England expelled him. The Gypsy might steal an occasional child or horse and hide successfully in a neighboring forest, fearing only wolves and boars, and then with the coming of autumn move south. A pirate could have his ship, his island sanctuary and his dream of booty.

But the hero of *The Little Golden Calf,* that prescient Bolshevik satire of 1924, could only look sadly at each village train station and say to himself "This is most assuredly not Rio de Janeiro." That man devoted his life to the fraudulant accumulation of a million rubles, but could find no place to spend them. One supposes he could with some effort have bought, over the years, a million copies of *Anna Karenina* and thrown them into Lake Baikal, but not much more.

Not only is today's wave of collectivism more complete than its predecessor, but the remaining seed of its alternative falls on ever stonier soil. Technology alone in its modern advance assures this result; indeed I believe it assures in the long run the ultimate and permanent victory of the collective ideal.

The pity is that the collective is what most people want. Even when freedom is greatest, in Jane Austen's England, or Sinclair Lewis' *Mainstreet,* we can observe the way people who could have done otherwise rush together to get each other's approval and to revile and punish the misfit. In a true legal collective--in the Massachusetts of Increase Mather--that misfit had no rights and was put to death. In liberal America the misfit had a vote and a bank account, could sell his house and move out of town; but still he could be made to suffer, even be hounded to death. Read Dreiser, read Ring Lardner: Even the liberal society has its lust for community, never entirely put down.

Imagine, then, a society where leaving town or leaving the country is as futile a move towards anonymity as moving next door would have been on Lewis' *Mainstreet.* Consider what we now have in the way of convenience: credit cards, drivers' licences, tax receipts, liability insurance. The mail, the telephone and finally the computer have made it possible for us to combine all our discrete identities under one great Identification Number. Social security, workman's compensation, Medicare, bank deposit and monthly payments can all be made on the same pushbutton keyboard that can print out our photograph, fingerprints and credit ratings.

What would the medieval manor have done with all this? What news could the troubador have brought from the next county that was not already known? His arrival would have been no surprise, and his songs but a rough version of the latest discs on the radio. With piracy put down and shipwreck practically unknown, how could proud merchants arise? Getters of goods would have been only another class of vassal.

This time around we will have the ability to accomplish and enforce what has always been the true majority desire. "'Tis the final conflict." Quite so, final because overwhelming.

Individual liberty has, after all, been a rare phenomenon in human history. A few people in Europe, during a couple of relatively brief stretches of time. Compared to the millennia of Egyptian and Babylonian formalism, the "cycles of Cathay", they have been but a moment, and an accidental moment at that. Very likely the ants and bees had such moments at some time in their own evolution, before they found happiness in its final form.

No more vested interests. Power to the people. Peace.